NEVER SETTLE FOR LESS

By
KESHA COX

Open Door Publications

Never Settle for Less
By Kesha M. Cox

Copyright © 2015 by Kesha M. Cox
ISBN: 978-0-9960985-5-7

All rights reserved.
Printed in the United States

No part of this book may be used or reproduced in any manner whatsoever without the written permission of the author except in the case of brief quotations embodied in critical articles and reviews.

All biblical references are taken from the New Believers Bible, New Living Translation, Greg Laurie, general editor, Tyndale House Publishers, copyright 1996.

The events told in this book are the author's memories of events. Some names have been changed to protect the privacy of the people involved.

Cover Design by Myesha Price, Designs By My, LLC

Published by
Open Door Publications
2113 Stackhouse Dr.
Yardley, PA 19067
www.OpenDoorPublications.com

DEDICATION

I dedicate this book to my beautiful mother, Katrina Renee Williams. You are the reason I am here today. No words can describe how much I love you and appreciate you for allowing me to be born. You will never be forgotten as long as I live. I love you, Mom.
Katrina Renee Williams, March 3, 1963–January 28, 1979

I also dedicate this book to my beloved grandparents Roscoe and Elizabeth Williams. I learned so much from watching you both live your lives in front of me. I am the woman I am today because of you. Thank you for being a living expression of family, devotion, wisdom, kindness, friendship, and thoughtfulness in my life. Your words of wisdom and love will always surround my heart. Thank you for raising and loving me. I am honored to be your granddaughter.
Elizabeth Williams, April 4, 1922–April 30, 1993
Roscoe Williams Sr., June 24, 1920–September 27, 2008

Table of Contents

Foreword i
1. Katrina 1
2. Derrick 8
3. Growing Pains 12
4. A New Experience 20
5. The Downward Spiral 28
6. Is It Worth It? 32
7. Be Yourself, Everyone Else is Taken 37
8. Friendly Conversations 45
9. Let the Game Begin 51
10. Looks Can be Deceiving 58
11. Watch Out for Traps 67
12. The C Word 70
13. I Should Have Listened 73
14. Never Settle for Less 82
15. Grandma 89
16. The C Word Again 94
17. Missing You 100
18. A Time for Everything 104
19. A Mother's Love 117
20. Lord, Help Me, I'm Drowning 121
21. Was it Worth Waiting? 125
22. Something Strange is Happening 131
23. When it All Ended 134
24. Life or Death 139
25. Call Me David 147
26. Going to the Chapel of Love 152
27. Acknowledgements 157

Foreword

Never Settle for Less is an amazing story of overcoming circumstances beyond your control, bad decisions, and the influence of the wrong people in your life. Kesha Cox has lived it, and by the grace of our Lord and Savior, she has taken the lessons of a long, winding journey, learned well from them, and has come to a resting place victorious.

Hers is a story of how Christ watches out for you, your safety, your family, even when you are on that longsuffering route that eventually leads you to him. The love of grandparents when you are orphaned; the protection of unseen angels when your judgment was flawed; the shelter of the Lord's loving arms when those closest to you put you and your children in harm's way, all are proof of the living God and his promise found in Romans 8:28, *"And we know that all things work together for good to them that love God, to them who are the called according to his purpose."*

Kesha suffered the process. She kept living life when it was almost unbearable and there was little hope in sight. She found that still small voice within that gave her the strength to carry on, to push through, to overcome what seemed to be the insurmountable. Today, her life is so much different than it was a short time ago. She has a loving husband. Her family is knit together. She is at a place where she can speak of those hopeless moments and give hope and encouragement to others.

Never Settle for Less is inspiring. It brings you through the vivid reality of times, decisions and situations with which we all can identify. It delivers us to the determination that neither death, nor life, nor principalities, nor anything whatsoever can separate us from the love of God. He, through his marvelous light, restores what has been destroyed by the locusts of life. Kesha's testimony assists us all in concluding we should Never Settle for Less.

Troy Vincent

1. Katrina

A mother's love can never be broken, even if she is far away. It is a shield that can never be moved, her love for me sings from above, "Baby Girl, I will see you soon."

My father met my mother one afternoon in downtown Trenton. My mother, Katrina, was thirteen years old, and Derrick, my father, wasn't much older.

ಬಂಡ

"Come out! Come out and fight me. I'm going to beat you real good for spitting on me," the girl shouted at the top of her voice.

"That's the funniest thing I ever saw," Derrick laughed to his friends, as they rode their bikes through Trenton Commons one summer afternoon.

The girl was only about five feet, three inches tall, and Derrick particularly noticed her long brown hair and big bright eyes. The woman inside the booth was large in size, and towered over the tiny girl in height, but she seemed terrified by her fierceness. Sweat and tears ran down the girl's face as she raged at the woman, demanding she come out of the telephone booth.

"That little girl doesn't look like she could hurt a fly, but she has a voice like a drill sergeant," Derrick told his friend. "We'd better help this woman from out of this telephone booth or that girl is going to hurt her."

The friend, rather reasonably, suggested they not get involved, and when Derrick waded into the middle of the situation, his friend quickly departed.

"What can I do to make you stop screaming and banging on that telephone booth so that terrified woman can go home?" Derrick asked.

Angrily, the girl turned toward Derrick and screamed, "Nothing! There's nothing you can do or say to me that's going to stop me from beating on this woman. She spit on me, and I'm going to get her real good for it."

Derrick was more intrigued than ever, and less inclined to leave; he wanted to know more about her. "If I buy you some pizza, would you leave her alone?"

"No!" she shouted, then paused to think. "Okay, but you have to buy me two slices of pizza and an orange soda or I'm going to wait until she comes out of this telephone booth and beat on her."

Derrick agreed. Katrina, which was the girl's name, he learned, screamed at the woman once again, kicked the telephone booth, and headed with him to the pizza shop around the corner. As he looked back he saw the terrified woman running down the street, leaving her bags behind. He laughed again saying, "That's the funniest thing I ever saw."

From that day on they became the best of friends. They would meet in the park after school and play, laugh, and joke around. They often went to the pizza shop together; in fact, they did almost everything together.

"Katrina is the best thing that ever happened to me. When I'm with her nothing else seems to matter," Derrick told his friends.

☙❦

Katrina was a fighter at heart; she fought for what she believed in. She did not take any nonsense from anyone, not even her sisters or brothers. She was loved by the many people who took the time to know her, but misunderstood by others because she had challenges; she often had seizures due to having meningitis at nine months old.

"Your mother almost died, Kesha, but with the help of many doctors and prayers she survived," my aunt would tell me. Katrina's seizures led her to confusion, which caused negative behavior. But to her family, and my father, she was a beautiful person, inside and out.

My mother and father were teenagers, and so inevitably, they fell in love. My mother was just fourteen years old when I was born, and while many people will say that she was a child having a child, my family soon realized it was the best thing that ever happened to her.

"When your mother told me she was pregnant, I was so upset with her," my grandmother said. "But she insisted she was not going to get rid of her baby, because she knew you were going to be special." Having a child changed my mother for the better in many ways. She was no longer quick to get angry and fight people. The little things, like kids calling her names and teasing her, seemed to not bother her as much because her concern was taking care of me.

My mother attended the Delaware Valley School for Exceptional Children, which provided children with special education services and care. Many of the other children in the neighborhood picked on her and teased her because they knew she went to that school.

"God knew what He was doing when He brought you into her life—and your father's, too," Grandma would say.

Kesha Cox

My mother wasn't alone in raising and taking care of me. She had seven sisters, two brothers, my grandparents, and of course, my father. He was a part of my life even though, because they were so young, they had not married. I was indeed in good, reliable hands.

But about a year and a half later, tragedy occurred. My mother drowned at the YWCA pool on Academy Street in Trenton. She was pulled unconscious from the pool, which was being watched by a swimming instructor and two counselors. The newspaper article stated the three gave her mouth-to-mouth resuscitation and a life mobile crew also gave first aid before she was rushed to the hospital. After hours of working on her, the doctors informed my grandparents that she only had forty-eight hours to live. A pathologist for the Mercer County Medical Examiner said his autopsy disclosed that cardiorespiratory insufficiency and cerebral damage caused her death: in other words, drowning. She was only fifteen years old.

When my father heard, he remembered something she often told him: "Derrick, I feel like I'm going to die young."

"I always told her not to talk that way, and your grandfather did, too," my father said. "He would say, 'Derrick, don't listen to that crazy talk Katrina is talking. Only God knows when we are going to leave this earth.'"

But my mother still believed it. She knew in her heart, she told my father, that she was going to die young.

My family, and of course my father, were devastated by my mother's death. She died at 7:50 a.m., on Sunday, January 28, 1979, at Helene Fuld Medical Center in Trenton.

Words can't describe how my father felt. He was grieving and confused. "I felt as if every bone in my body was broken and crushed into a million tiny pieces. Part of me was gone with her. And I was terrified at the thought of raising a baby on my own," he told me.

He decided to allow my grandparents to raise me and joined the Marines to make a living for us.

"There was never a doubt in my mind that I was going to raise you as my own when your mother died," my grandmother always said. "God took your mother away, but He gave me you."

Grandma had a special gift; she was able to discern certain things that were going to happen in someone's life. She often knew when someone was pregnant or when someone was going to die. She had had a dream a few years earlier, she told me, and she saw two of her daughters dead but she couldn't see their faces.

Her youngest daughter, Katrina, was dead, and just two years later tragedy struck again. My mother's sister, Barbara, died from a blood clot in her lung on April 16, 1981. She was twenty-six years old. My grandparents' hearts had not healed from the loss of one daughter, how could they stand the pain of burying two daughters two years apart from each other?

☙❧

Even with my father and grandparents by my side, I often would ask myself how life would have been if my mother was still here. Would she have married my father eventually? Would I have had a sister or brother? Would we have been the best of friends? What would life be like if my mommy was still with me? Those questions went unanswered, and many nights I would sit in the corner of my room crying out for her to come back home and be with me. I would hold a picture of my mother holding me, and for a few hours, as I slept through the night, I was comforted. But when I woke up in the morning and only had the picture of her holding me, and not her physical presence, I felt devastated all over again.

The many pictures I had of my mother holding me and kissing me were wonderful and meant so much to me, but I would never know how she truly felt—the warmth of her skin, her kiss, her touch, her voice, her hugs. There was no doubt in my mind that she had loved me, but I wanted to hear her say it. I wanted to hear her voice say those four little words, "Kesha, I love you."

Over the years, I would often pray and ask God to help me in my struggle to deal with my mother's passing. There was a part of me that had died with her even though I didn't remember her. There was a void in my heart that was empty. Yes, I know that God makes no mistakes, but why my mother? One of my biggest sorrows was that one day, when I got married, I would have no one to experience those special moments of helping me prepare for my wedding. Who would be there by my side to watch me give birth to my children? Who would talk to me about becoming a woman? I wanted those mommy and daughter discussions, those nights where I could cry, laugh, and lay my head on her shoulder and just talk about anything.

Grandma always said God never takes something away without replacing it. I didn't understand those words then but I understand them now. God replaced that which he took away with loving, caring, and supportive grand-parents, a father who adored me, and a family who loved me. God in time filled that empty void that only He could fill in me. My mother will never be forgotten, and she will always hold a special place in my heart. Grandma always said everything that we go through in life is always working out for our good even when it doesn't look like it.

Never Settle for Less

Romans 8:28: And we know that all things work together for good to those who love God and are called according to His purpose.

2. Derrick

God will fill the voids and heal the hurt all because His love is sufficient for all our needs.

My father was often away while he was in the Marines, but he was still a presence in my life. Whenever he came home to visit me, he would always bring me something special. He never came to see me empty-handed, even though as I got older he knew that the gifts were never as important as his presence. He made my day every time he came around. It was like staring at beautiful fireworks in the sky when he walked through the door. "Hello, Sweetheart," or "Hello, Dear," he would say as he hugged and kissed me. He always made sure my grandparents had what they needed to care for me. Many people think that if a man isn't physically present for his children every day he is a deadbeat dad. But, not my father. He was a loving and caring father who wanted the best for his child.

I will never forget the day my grandmother sat me on her lap and told me that my father wouldn't be able to come to see me for a long time. She explained that because of something he had done that was not right, he would not be able to come by the house to see me. I burst into tears.

"Why? Why? Why?" I cried so hard I couldn't even get that one word out clearly. Why would he not want to see me? Why would he not want to come by to pick me up and take me places? What had I done to make him leave me?

My grandmother held me tight in her arms, rocking me back and forth saying, "Kesha, there are some things we will never understand, but I promise I will make sure you speak with your father any time he calls. I will make sure you visit him every time you can."

That entire day I clung tightly to my grandmother. Wherever she went in the house, I followed her. I was afraid of letting her out of my sight, fearing she, too, would not return.

My father was everything to me, and I couldn't imagine life without him. But now he was gone, and it was as if life was repeating itself all over again. My mother was gone, and my father had to serve time in prison. Who was going to walk out of my life next? The pain of losing my parents was unbearable. I would often just sit in a corner of my bedroom crying, praying, and pleading with God to stop removing the people I needed in my life.

I would panic whenever new people came into my life because I was afraid they would also leave. I would put up a wall of defense, so they wouldn't get close to me and hurt me, or I would cling to them, never wanting them to leave. My grandmother would notice my many emotions and attachment to people, and she would spend more time with me, talking to me and embracing me with her love. Often as we sat in the front yard of our house, my grandmother would say, "There will always be people who come in and out our lives, for many different reasons. You have to enjoy the time and special moments you are allowed to spend with them. There is a season and time for everything." I didn't understand those words at that time, but I surely do now.

As she shared pictures and special moments of my mother and father, she would say, "Always remember they loved you, and remember there was nothing they wouldn't do for you."

My grandparents were major figures in my life, especially my grandmother. They didn't want anyone to hurt me. They knew how much my father meant to me, so they found ways for me to visit him and talk to him over the phone. He would call every week to see how I was doing, and my eyes lit up every time that phone rang. I shared everything with him about school, my friends, and how much I missed him.

He was a kind, loving, and a gentle man in spite of what he had done.

"Sweetheart, always remember you can talk to me about anything. I will never stop loving you or being there for you," he told me, and I held those words close to my heart. Although he wasn't there physically, he never stopped being a father to me. The same love I had felt when he walked through the front door was the same love I felt when he called me over the phone, and that was the best feeling a little girl could ask for.

My grandparents kept him in the loop on every stage of my life. He never skipped a beat when it came to me. He was a part of every discussion about school, discipline, friends, boyfriends, even to the day I graduated from high school. We would pray, laugh, and cry over the phone as if he was sitting next to me. He was always supportive of any decision I made, from the time I was a little girl until I grew into a young adult. I am grateful for the support and close relationship we have to this day.

My father realized he had made a great mistake and was

willing to face his responsibilities so that he could come back home to be with me. The day that he was released from prison he stepped back into my life.

With time, understanding, and maturity, I learned that God will give you what you need in order to continue on with life. He gave me a father who loved me and two beautiful grandparents who took on the role of mother and father.

Psalm 27:10: Even if my father and mother abandon me, the Lord will hold me close.

3. Growing Pains

I was in captivity to the words "stupid, dumb, slow, retarded, not good enough and learning disability." I let those words define me as a person.

"Mrs. Walker, I need to take Kesha for some testing."

The tiny lady who had walked into my third grade classroom with a bunch of folders in her hands was about to change my life, but at the time, all I wondered was why I was being singled out.

"Kesha, take your things and go with this lady," Mrs. Walker said.

"For what?" I responded nervously.

"I need to test you in certain subjects to see how well you understand the work," the lady responded.

Those were the worst words I could have heard. Though she spoke softly and directly to me, the entire class heard her. They all laughed so loudly that Mrs. Walker had to tell them to be quiet.

"They got to take you to a special class because you can't keep up in here," one boy shouted.

I wanted to die. I started to cry and pleaded with the lady not to take me. "I don't need to be tested. I understand. I know I do. Sometimes it just takes me longer, but I'm fine.

Really."

My crying didn't change anything, of course. The lady and Mrs. Walker just took me into the hall to calm me down.

"You're not in trouble, Kesha. And there's nothing wrong with you. Everyone just learns and comprehends things differently. You are just going to take a test to see how you learn and comprehend information. It doesn't mean you are not smart. It just means that you may need extra help in certain areas of study."

Her words warmed my heart with hope and encouragement, and I followed the lady, who I learned was named Ms. Allen, into her classroom where she began to test me. She made me feel relaxed by explaining to me that I should answer all the questions the best way I knew how, and she encouraged me, telling me I was going to do great. That was all I needed to hear, "You are going to do great!" I sat in that chair and focused and concentrated on every question, and I knew within my heart that I was going to prove to Ms. Allen and Mrs. Walker I didn't need to be tested or have a teacher's aide to work with me in the classroom, because I was smart just like the other kids.

About two weeks later Ms. Allen came back into the classroom and requested I come with her. Once again my classmates started to laugh and crack jokes, saying that I was going into a retarded classroom for the slow learners.

This time I didn't cry. I just turned around and looked at them all and said, "Well, I guess you all should just be following me." The class got very quiet, and Mrs. Walker quickly looked at me from the corner of her eye and gently smiled. As I walked with Ms. Allen to her classroom, I was very nervous. I didn't know what she would say about the tests I had taken. She could tell I was worried. "Don't be so nervous. Everything is going to be fine," she said as we walked down the hall. I smiled at her.

Ms. Allen told me to have a seat and relax while she looked for my test scores.

"You didn't do too badly, but you do need extra help in math, language arts, and reading, and I may recommend some speech therapy classes because I noticed you have a hard time pronouncing a few words. But I'm going to help you." Ms. Allen was right, some words I did have a hard time pronouncing, which was why I was always embarrassed to read out loud in class or sometimes talk to people.

I felt sad as she spoke, because I had wanted to hear her say I had done great and there was no need for me to have resource classes or a teacher's aide to assist me. But Ms. Allen was persistent in encouraging me; she told me that she, too, had had a hard time understanding and comprehending certain information when she was in school, but it didn't mean she was not smart or any different from the other kids. It just meant she had to work extra hard and do her best to stay on top of her grades and studies.

"I had a teacher's aide who would come into the classroom to help me in math, reading, and language arts. She encouraged me and inspired me to work and study hard, and I want to do the same for you. She told me she wanted me to know I could become whatever my little heart desired," Ms. Allen said.

"And that's what I did. I worked hard and did my best in everything, and I produced great results. And because of the words of my teacher's aide and the people who believed in me, I am now a teacher who is able to help children who have learning disabilities."

"A learning disability!" I shouted. "What does that mean?"

Ms. Allen gently smiled and explained to me that it

NEVER SETTLE FOR LESS

didn't mean that I was sick in any way. It meant that I had some difficulty learning in certain areas, but with some help and support I would do fine. Ms. Allen said she would talk to my grandparents to discuss more details and sent me back to class.

I felt as if my whole world was ending before it ever got started. How could I have a learning disability? Sure, I struggled in some subjects, but didn't everyone? I wasn't dumb. *"Now the kids are really going to laugh at me once they find out I need a teacher's aide to help with my class assignments,"* I thought. This was so embarrassing, I couldn't face my classmates laughing in my face and talking behind my back.

After school I went straight home and asked Grandma if I was born with any birth defects.

"No, you silly girl," she laughed. "What are you talking about?"

"The school gave me some tests to take, and they said I was dumb. Now I have to have a teacher's aide in the classroom and speech therapy classes."

"Oh Kesha, you silly girl. I knew all about those tests before you took them, and trust me, the school is only trying to help you. You see, we all have some type of problems, Baby. It doesn't mean we are less of a person. You were made just the way God wanted you to be. It's nothing wrong with you; you just need a little help and support in certain areas. Ms. Allen and Mrs. Walker are going to see to it that you get that extra help, but you have to be open to receive what they are offering to you."

"But Mom," (this is what I called my grandmother), "the kids are going to laugh and crack jokes when they find out, and I don't want to hurt nobody. You know how I get when I get angry."

KESHA COX

"Oh girl, go sit down! You sound just like your mother when the kids used to tease her. You just got to prove to yourself that you can do whatever you put your heart to do. You just have to focus and work a little harder, Baby."

"I know, Mom, but I hate being different, I want to be normal,"

"But you are normal, as normal as you are ever going to be. God didn't create no junk when it came to you, me, and everybody else. We are just a little different, and being different is sometimes good."

Grandma saw that I still felt a little uncomfortable talking about the test, so she held out her hand for me to grab, then gently squeezed my hand and said, "You see, Kesha, God created you with everything that you need to accomplish whatever you want to do. Just believe in yourself a little, Baby, and I will always be there to help you as much as I can."

It sounded fine when my grandmother or Ms. Allen or Mrs. Walker told me I just work a little different than others and just needed some extra help in a few areas. But the reality of being a kid in school is different.

ಣಚ

"Hey Kesha, what's two plus two?"

"How do you spell A?"

All the kids were laughing and pointing their fingers at me as I walked into the classroom. It happened all the time. Not just in third grade, but in fourth and fifth and sixth grades, too. It never got any better. I would become so angry that I shouted back. "Two plus two equals four and an A is an A but add two more letters after the A and let me know what you come up with!"

The kids started laughing because they knew what the other two letters spelled, so the joke was no longer on me it

Never Settle for Less

was on them—and "them" usually meant Ralph, the shortest, and meanest, bully in the school.

"Good morning, boys and girls."

"Good morning, Mrs. Walker," the class shouted back.

"After I take attendance I'm going to have a talk with the class about some of the inappropriate things I've been hearing around the school about other students."

"Oh boy," I thought, *"Now Ralph and everyone are going to get in trouble for teasing me."*

I was right.

"We're in trouble because of you," Ralph shouted across the room at me. "You must of gone home and cried to your grandma."

"No, I didn't, so shut up, and if you keep running your big mouth I'm going to knock you across your face." I was mad and angry and now I wanted to FIGHT!

"Now Kesha," Mrs. Walker said, "we don't act like that in this classroom. If you have a problem, then you need to talk to me after school and we can settle the issue."

"Well, we can settle this issue now!"

"Excuse me, Kesha, you will not talk to me in that tone of voice."

"I'm tired of the kids teasing me. I'm not dumb, I'm not stupid. I just work a little different than the others," I repeated what the adults had all told me, with tears running down my face.

"You are right, Kesha, you are far from dumb. You are very bright and smart, and no one in this class will be made fun of, because everyone learns differently. If I catch anyone talking or laughing about anyone's learning abilities, I will call your parents and request a meeting. Do I make myself clear?"

"Yes, Mrs. Walker."

It felt so good to get that out of my system, I felt that Mrs. Walker had come to my defense, and after class I told her I was sorry for yelling at her, but I was angry and frustrated by what the kids were saying about me.

"Just don't let it happen again. Kesha, you should be very grateful for the help you are receiving from myself, Ms. Allen, and your grandparents. We care a lot about you, and we want to see you improve in every subject and become a great person someday. Though it may be hard ignoring the jokes and teasing of your classmates, know that we have your best interest at heart, and you will someday look back over your life and appreciate the gifts we truly are to you."

I looked into Mrs. Walker's eyes with tears running down my face and said, "Thank you, someday I am going to be just like you."

Over the course of the years, even through high school, I encountered many challenges from peers who didn't understand and mistreated me because of my learning disability, and because of who I was as a person. I was called the kid from Special Ed. I was very quiet and shy but would offer my friendship and love to anyone who would take the time to know me. I enjoyed staying to myself. I didn't like to be around a lot of people because I was afraid they would notice my problem. My grandma would say, "The less friends you have, the better off you are."

I agreed with Grandma, but it was hard and lonely being made fun of. I would stay around my grandmother and her friends because I felt safe with them. I didn't have to worry about them pointing the finger at me, or laughing and cracking jokes.

Learning and comprehending things on a different level than my peers were very hard for me to accept, no matter how many times I was encouraged and inspired by my

Never Settle for Less

teachers and loved ones to become my best. I felt I was less of a person, having no value, and would always have to settle for the lesser things in life. Whether I was applying for a summer job, meeting new people, participating in school or outside activities, or building relationships, I felt that everyone could see my weakness and that they would judge me for it. So instead of being friendly and approachable, I rejected others before they could reject me. I kept quiet, kept to myself, and avoided unnecessary contact.

I was in captivity to the words "stupid, dumb, slow, retarded, not good enough, and learning disability." I let those words define me as a person. I felt I had no value so I had no self-love, and my self-esteem was low. I felt inadequate in everything that I put my hands to. I was a poor judge of character when it came to dating or choosing the right friends, which led to many of my downfalls. I settled for less. But with time, self-evaluation, forgiveness, determination, hope, and love, I came to know that I was different for a reason and filled with purpose.

Psalm 139:13-14: You made all the delicate inner parts of my body and knit me together in my mother's womb. Thank you for making me so wonderfully complex.

4. A NEW EXPERIENCE

*Be mindful of what you open yourself up to,
because it could be a trap.*

School was ending and summertime was approaching; it was time for me to take a break from all the teasing, joking, and name-calling by the kids in school. I was relieved to enjoy a summer of fun with my family and friends around my neighborhood. I was thirteen years old and nobody could tell me nothing. I was becoming a young lady in my eyes, but Grandma's eyes saw things differently.

"Kesha!"

"Yes, Mom, what do you want?" I shouted.

"Girl, you better watch how you talk to me in that tone of voice or I will give you just what you are looking for."

"Okay, okay, Mom," I said sulkily. "I'm sorry, but you keep calling my name every five minutes while I am trying to have fun with my friends."

"Well, I keep calling your name every five minutes because you're not answering me when I call you."

"I'm sorry, Mom, but I'm trying to have fun with my

Never Settle for Less

friends while it's still light outside."

"When the streetlights come on you better be on this front porch where I can see you."

"Are you serious? Why do I have to be on the porch when the streetlights come on? It's not like I have to go to school the next day."

"Because I said so!"

"You make me sick!" I yelled.

"I make you what?"

As soon as the words were out of my mouth I was running up the front porch with tears pouring down my face, pleading with my grandmother to stop spanking me. Every time she would swing the belt in my direction she would say, "You better not ever talk to me like that again, do you hear me?"

And every time she said those words I quickly responded "yes" so the spanking would stop. The entire night seemed like it would never end.

I felt horrible about how I had spoken to my grandmother. I knew she meant well and only wanted what was best for me. But part of me felt as if she didn't want me to grow up. I thought she was overbearing, always wanting me to be in her sight and reach. I was too young and too immature to understand that she only had my best interest in mind. She knew what was out there waiting for young girls like me, and she would do anything to protect me and keep me safe.

Before the morning sun came up the next day I tiptoed to her bedroom door and whispered softly, "Mom, Mom, are you awake?"

"No, child, what are you doing up so early?"

"I just wanted to say I was sorry for talking to you that way yesterday."

"Okay. We will talk later. Now go back to bed."

Later that day we did talk. When she called me I walked toward her rocking chair with my heart pounding so hard it could have jumped out of my chest. "*Lord, please help me,*" I prayed. I didn't know what she was going to do or say.

"Huh? I mean, yes?"

"Listen to what I'm about to tell you, and I want you to listen good. When I tell you to do something I expect you to listen and follow my instructions. If you won't follow my instructions then maybe I need to find some other place for you to live."

"No, Mom. I don't want to live anywhere else. I want to stay here with you and Daddy" (my grandfather).

"Well, if you don't get yourself together, you going to find yourself out those doors. I'm too old to deal with this mess."

"Okay, Mom, I understand."

ಬಿಲ

Grandma often told me that there were a lot of terrible things out there in those streets just waiting to get ahold of me—especially little girls like me who didn't know any better.

"Those streets will swallow you up alive if you're not careful, Baby. You are still young and there's a lot of things you need to learn, but the only way to learn is to listen and follow instructions."

And I would reply, "I know, Mom, I know," hoping to make her quickly change the conversation. Was I listening to her advice? Yes. But there was also always that feeling in my heart that she just didn't understand how I felt.

But Grandma was no fool. She was very sensitive to people's feelings; she knew what they were going through even before they could tell her.

NEVER SETTLE FOR LESS

She knew what I was thinking or what I was about to do, and she always had the right words to say. Sometimes she would warn me about things I was just thinking about doing—even when I hadn't done them yet. Was Grandma some type of mind reader who could read people's thoughts? No, but she was my angel sent from God to raise and take care of me.

She knew I struggled with wanting to feel accepted by my peers. I often felt I wasn't equal to my peers, not even to some of my cousins. I wanted to feel special and unique. I wanted people to recognize and take notice of me and not my learning disability. *Would people accept me as I was?* That is the question I would often ask myself. But the sad part was I didn't even accept myself. I thought I had to be like everyone else: smart, intelligent, and beautiful. The reality was I was all of those things; I just didn't know it.

Feeling different didn't feel good. I felt lonely and often afraid. Would I ever stop thinking less of myself? Grandma would always say, "If you don't love yourself, nobody on this earth will, and you will always settle for the lesser of everything." But I was too young to understand. I desperately longed for someone to notice and accept me and not notice my issue.

ಊಡಣ

One afternoon as I sat on the porch a friend came into the yard and asked if I wanted to play kick ball in the back parking lot where we always played our outdoor games.

"Yeah, okay," I responded, so we played kick ball along with other kids on our street. Our team of five girls beat the boys' team of seven. We were so hyped that day nobody could tell us nothing. We were Faircrest winners!

"Kesha, what are you doing when you get home?" my friend asked.

"Nothing. I'll probably help my grandma prepare dinner. Why?"

"Because I have something I need to show you at my house, so just tell your grandma you are coming to my house, okay?"

I was so anxious to know what she wanted to show me that I kept asking her as we walked, but all she said was, "Just be quiet and promise you won't tell anybody."

"Okay," I promised. "I won't."

We walked into the house and nobody was home. "Where is your mom and dad? If my grandma finds out they're not here, I can get into trouble."

"Nobody is going to get into trouble. If you would just be quiet no one will know."

We went downstairs in the basement; she turned on the TV and put a tape in the VCR. "Are you ready for this?" she asked.

She pushed the play button, and there on the screen were people having sex and doing all sorts of things to each other.

"Oh my goodness! Turn this off before we get into trouble!" I said.

"Be quiet before somebody hears you. Just watch and maybe we can learn something from this for when we start to meet boys."

My mouth said okay, even though my heart knew it was wrong. I kept trying to make myself turn my head and walk away, but my eyes stayed glued to the television set. I had never seen anything like this before. Of course I had heard about sex, I knew what it was, but hearing people talk about it was very different from actually seeing it.

Sex was something we never talked about in our household. Grandma stayed away from that topic, and because she stayed away, I didn't mention it to her or

Never Settle for Less

anybody else. I was too young to be having sex anyway, and I was sure that no one would ever be interested in having sex with me. So the entire time I watched that sex tape I nervously paced the floor. I felt so uncomfortable, but I kept telling myself to sit down and relax, to stay calm. "Everything is going to be all right," I told myself. "People have sex every day, and besides this is something I have to learn eventually."

"Kesha, promise me you are not going to tell anybody that we were watching this tape," my friend said.

"Okay, I promise I won't say anything," I said as I approached the front door. As I stepped outside I heard my grandmother calling my name. I ran toward home as if two pit bulls were chasing me because I didn't want to get into trouble.

"Child, I have been calling your name for the last five minutes. Where were you?"

"I was in the park on the swings, Mom. I'm sorry."

"Okay, well go and wash your hands and get ready for dinner."

The entire time I sat at the dinner table all I could think about was the images on that sex tape. For the life of me I couldn't get those images out of my mind.

"Kesha, Kesha," my grandma called me twice, but I did not hear her. "Child, go and call your grandfather in for dinner. He's out there in the field."

"Okay, Mom." I wanted to tell her the truth about where I had been, but I had made my friend a promise. I wouldn't tell because I knew we would get into trouble.

"Kesha, you have been daydreaming since you came into the house. What's wrong, Baby?"

"Nothing, Mom, nothing."

"I know when something is wrong with my baby. Tell

me what it is."

"Nothing, Mom, please, there's nothing wrong with me."

The truth was something was wrong. I couldn't shake the images I had seen on that sex tape. It kept playing in my head. The next day we were all outside playing jump rope, having a good time, and my friend asked me again if I wanted to come over and watch the tape with her. I said "okay," but this time all I could hear in my mind was Grandma saying, "You'd better be mindful of what you open yourself up to, because it could be a trap."

I didn't listen. I put her voice way in the back of my head and walked to my friend's house. We sat and watched the tape for about an hour before it was time for me to go home.

"This tape will teach us everything that we need to learn about what boys like, and we will never be without a boyfriend," my friend told me as I got ready to leave.

"But what about the things we like?"

"Girl, we first need to think about what satisfies them before we can think about what satisfies us."

It was what she had heard her mother say, and what she had heard from television and music. But it wasn't what I had heard at home. I was confused and didn't know what to believe. Was sex just for the boys to be satisfied?

"Remember, Kesha, you better not tell anybody or I will never talk to you again," she said as I left the house.

"Okay, I won't," I promised once again.

Why did I not listen to my grandmother's advice to be mindful of what I opened myself up to? It could be a trap that would control my every thought, action, and words, a trap that would leave an imprint on my heart and lead me to do things I knew weren't right.

I couldn't shake the images I'd seen, and they ran like a tape recorder in my mind, playing over and over again. I opened my mind and heart to a world of sex I wasn't ready for without a clue of the impact it would have on my life years down the road.

1 Corinthians 15:33: Don't be fooled by those who say such things for "bad company corrupts good character."

5. The downward spiral

I knew I shouldn't settle for less, but what was the "more" I should be looking for?

As I approached middle school I watched the other girls to see how they dressed and acted with each other and the boys, and I used that as a guide to prepare myself for what was to come. I knew it was time for a change; I was becoming older and wanted to feel part of something instead of distant all the time. I began to hang around the girls who were somewhat popular and had their own style. I had always drawn others to me with my big bright smile and quietness. I loved to smile because it made me feel better about myself, and my grandmother loved to see me smile. She said that I had a smile that was warm and welcoming. Now, I used my smile and meekness to my advantage to make friends and draw attention to myself.

I didn't realize it at the time, but I drew friends who needed someone to confide in, because they knew that I could be trusted. It made me feel special that others could talk to me and tell me their secrets without them feeling judged. I learned years later others can often see the uniqueness and special character traits that we overlook in ourselves. I was beginning to be accepted by others, especially those who had rejected me in the past. I took on the role of counselor, the person everyone wanted to confide in.

I had a few friends, especially boys. I started changing the way I dressed and tried to look more sophisticated by wearing makeup. I used some of the girls' styling techniques to grab the attention of the guys, and to my surprise, it worked. My entire physical appearance seemed to change overnight. Grandma was forced to get me a bigger bra size, and it seemed as if I was getting taller, thicker, and rounder by the day; everything about my physical appearance was changing and my attitude about how I viewed myself also changed. When I was younger, my grandmother and teachers had always told me I was beautiful on the inside; now I knew I was beautiful on the outside, too. I was becoming a young lady, and my behavior, instead of changing for the better, was slowly turning for the worst. One day when I was walking home from school, a group of boys from my class started talking about me as I walked in front of them.

"Look at Kesha with that big butt!"

"You looking good, girl, walking in front of us like that."

The more they talked, the faster I walked. I couldn't wait until I got home to tell my grandma.

I burst through the door yelling, "Mom, Mom!"

"Kesha, what are you yelling about?"

"Some boys were walking behind me saying all sorts of things about my butt and how I was shaped."

"Did they touch you?"

"No, but if they had the chance they would have."

"Well, don't worry about it. The one thing you are going to learn in this world of ours is, people are going to talk about you regardless of how you look. As long as they don't put their hands on you, you will be fine." Grandma continued, "Remember this, Baby, if your body is all they notice, then that's all they want."

I thought about Grandma's words. They were powerful and encouraging but, at the same time, I also thought about the words the boys were saying about me. Their words were playing like a tape in my mind and overpowered those of my grandmother. Because all I had ever experienced was my peers saying hurtful things about me, being noticed by the boys felt kind of good. I was confused. I felt good and bad at the same time. I knew I shouldn't settle for less, but what was the "more" I should be looking for?

I went to school the next day and shared the story with my friends. They were thrilled. They suggested that I wear clothes that were more formfitting to show off my shape and get even more attention. I took their advice and began to wear a little more makeup and buy jeans and shirts that fit my shape more snugly. Grandma knew I wanted to look older and feel a part of things, but if she'd known the real reason for the change, she'd have had something to say about it.

I was changing my style, and I was changing my friends. I sought out the girls who were known to be "boy-getters." They knew how to get a boyfriend and keep him—and I was interested in both. I wanted to be with the girls "who had it 'going on.'"

The more I changed physically and socially, the stricter my grandparents became. I wanted to hang outside after the streetlights came on. I wanted to go hang out in the park. I wanted to talk on the phone with boys more. I wanted to do a whole lot of stuff I wouldn't have done before I got noticed walking home from school that day. Every weekend I

Never Settle for Less

wanted to shop for clothes, and anyone who knew my grandparents knew they were not taking me shopping every week. They were on fixed incomes, the only income they both received on a monthly basis. So I asked my Grandma if I could get a job delivering newspapers around the neighborhood, and she agreed as long as I could get one of my cousins to help me.

I was so excited to be able to have my own money. Even though it wasn't that much, it was mine! I could now save up to shop and dress how I wanted. Peer pressure was real. Grandma always said if you let others define you and tell you your value, it could be costly to your reputation in the end. Your life will be filled with hopeless and unfulfilled dreams. But with time and maturity I grew to understand that sometimes sticking out in the crowd is okay.

Proverbs 3:1-4: My child never forget the things I have taught you. Store my commands in your heart for they will give you a long and satisfying life. Never let loyalty and kindness get away from you! Wear them like a necklace; write them deep within your heart. Then you will find favor with both God and people, and you will gain a good reputation.

6. Is it worth it?

Are the people you are trying to impress going to be around when you need them? Likely not. Is it worth risking everything you believe in just to be accepted by your peers?

Compromising my integrity, going against what I was taught, and compromising who I was as a young lady—would it really cost me in the future? My grandmother told me it would, but I didn't believe her. Most of us don't when we are teenagers, but I learned the hard way.

Are the people I'm trying to impress going to be around when I need them the most? Likely not. Is it worth risking everything that I was taught and believed in just to be accepted by my peers?

I would ask myself these questions as I sat in the corner of my room staring at the wall. Was my life more than a one-night stand, or the talk of the streets? Yes, it was! But I didn't have the courage to say no, or turn the other way, and be my own person. A follower I was, but a leader I desired to be. It was going to take many mistakes, frustrations, and the disappointment of others for me to accept my leading role as a young lady who was called to be different, who believed that I was valuable and priceless.

I knew from conversations I heard at school that I was being noticed. I began to carry myself with pride; I was no longer afraid to talk to people. I no longer stood back and felt ashamed and scared if someone taunted me. I stood my ground and demanded respect. I wanted to be down with the crew. The only thing that was missing was a boyfriend, someone I could claim as my own. I needed my friends' advice. I had always been shy and nervous around boys, so if I was going to meet anyone it would be with the help of my friends.

Every day at lunchtime and walking home from school I listened to my friends talk about their boyfriends and how they kissed and hugged and how they managed to let their boyfriends hit home base. I would act as if I did not understand what they were talking about, but of course I did. I had watched those movies, after all. I knew what they were talking about. Part of me wanted to experience it, too, while another part of me didn't.

"What do y'all mean by letting your boyfriend hit home base?" I would ask.

"Don't be silly, Kesha, you know exactly what home base is—sex."

I wondered when they had the time to let anyone hit home base with their parents at home. What kind of parents allowed them to run the streets like they did, let alone have sex? That question was always in the back of my mind because my grandparents would never allow boys to come on our property unless they were neighborhood friends, and even they were sometimes limited to my front yard. My grandparents had to know you well before you could step foot onto their property. They were strict; they did not allow any nonsense to take place in their presence. They believed

Kesha Cox

"a child should always stay in a child's place," as my grandma would say. And at 14 years old, in our home, you had better stay in a child's place if you knew what was best for you.

I discovered over time that the reason my friends could go out with boys and have sex with them was because their parents were never home, usually because they were working, so the children were left alone and could do whatever they wanted. I didn't have that freedom. My grandparents were always home, and were always involved in everything that I did.

"Tonya, how would I go about dating when my grandparents are always around, and wanting to know my every move?" I asked one friend.

"You have to sneak and make up a story to tell your grandmother if you want to have a boyfriend. Just tell her you are going to a friend's house, then sneak off to see him."

"Are you crazy? Sneak off and lie to my grandparents? You're asking to never see me again."

"Oh Kesha, that's what all parents say when they try to keep their children in check. They look for ways to scare you. Stop being so scared and give it a try."

I liked a boy by the name of Allen Tucker. He was tall and handsome, with green bright eyes, and he was built like a football player, and all the girls loved themselves some Allen Tucker.

Allen was a ladies' man. One day as I walked down the hall to the main office to drop off some forms, he was coming out of the office.

"Hey Kesha, what's up?"

Oh my god he just said my name! After seconds of pausing in shock, I slowly turned around, smiled, and said, "Hi, Allen, how are you doing?"

As I slowly walked away, he turned his head and looked at me. I was on cloud nine all day long. For the rest of the day I rehearsed in my mind the moment Allen walked past me and said my name. I felt goose bumps all over my body; I was nervous. At the end of the school day I headed toward my locker to get my books, and there he was, hanging by my locker.

"Kesha, what's up with you? You looking good, girl. Would you like to go out and chill with me?"

"What? Are you for real?" I squeaked excitedly.

"Does it seem like I'm joking?"

"No, but where are we going to go? I can't be out late, so it's going to have be directly after school."

"Okay, that's fine. Do you like pizza?"

"Yes, I do."

"So let's go to the pizza shop across the street from the school."

"Okay, see you tomorrow after school." I was so excited. But, what was I going to tell my grandma? She was never going to go for it. The entire night I worried about it. If I was late coming home from school, she was going to put me on punishment. I called my friend Val, who was expert at setting up dates.

"Kesha, just tell your grandma you'll be staying after school with your teacher to work on some extra math work."

"But what if she asks the teacher if I stayed after school?"

"Just give her my number and I will act like Mrs. Smith. I mean I do sound like her a little bit."

"Okay, Val, but are you sure this is going to work?"

"Yes, if you stop being so nervous and scared."

I still talked myself out of the date with Allen about twenty times before I approached my grandma. After dinner

Kesha Cox

I did the oldest trick in the book. I ran into her arms and told her I loved her. "Love you more," she said, embracing me in return.

"Mom, can I stay after school to finish up some extra math work tomorrow? I want to get some extra credit." The entire time I was talking my eyes were across the room looking at the front door. I didn't dare look her in the face while I told her a lie.

"That's fine, but you better make sure that you come straight home afterwards."

"Are you sure, Grandma?" I stood twisting my thumbs.

"Yes, I'm sure, but you be careful walking home. There are crazy people out there. You don't want to be their prey."

Prey! Mom, you say the craziest things sometimes.

That night I tossed and turned, unable to believe I had just told my grandma, my best friend in the whole world, a lie. I was afraid of disappointing my grandparents. They had both sacrificed so much to raise me, and I was about to destroy their trust. Was it worth it? Was it worth hurting their hearts and disappointing them? The answer to that questions is "no." As I look back over my childhood, he wasn't worth losing their trust.

Proverbs 4:1-3: My children listen to me. Listen to your father's instruction. Pay attention and grow wise, for I am giving you good guidance. Don't turn away from my teaching. For I, too, was once my father's son, tenderly loved by my mother as an only child.

7. Be yourself, everyone else is taken

Each day when I wake up I have one more day to make a better decision concerning my life.

Birds were chirping and the sun was beaming through the window of my bedroom. *Oh my god is it time to get up?* As I remembered what had taken place the previous day my heart began to race. Anxious and nervous, I ran down the hall to Grandma's bedroom to tell her I didn't feel good and couldn't go to school.

"Kesha, what's wrong?"

"My head is hurting, Mom. I don't feel good. Please, Grandma, I don't want to go to school. Can I stay home, pleeease?"

"No way. You are getting out of this house today."

I burst into tears. "Grandma, please, I'm so sorry. I'm so sorry."

"What in the world are you talking about? Get in the shower and get ready for school. I'll get you some Advil and maybe you'll feel better."

As I entered the bathroom I heard her say under her breath, "This girl is losing her mind."

No, Grandma, you just don't know what's about to take place today, and I don't know how to get myself out of this mess I got myself into. God, please help me get out of this situation.

"Kesha, get out of that bathroom and get down these steps right now and take this medicine."

"Okay, Mom, I'm coming, please stop rushing me!"

I came downstairs holding my head and walked toward my grandma so that I could take my medicine and give her a kiss goodbye and reminded her that I was staying late after school.

"Okay, be careful."

As she said those words my heart fell to the floor. I wanted to tell her I wasn't being honest with her and that I was sorry for lying. But I couldn't because I was too ashamed. I walked out the door with my head down, hoping she would tell me to come back into the house and stay home.

The entire school day seemed so long; I could not wait until it was over.

"Kesha, are you ready for this afternoon with Allen?"

"No, I'm not, Val. I'm so nervous I just want to go home."

"Oh, stop being a baby," Val said. "Be a woman. We all had to go through this." I knew exactly what Val was talking about: having sex with Allen for the first time. I mean all the girls in my crew had sex with their boyfriends and seemed to be okay. But, in my mind we were still kids, and the thought of me having sex with him scared the life out of me. What if something happened, such as getting pregnant or catching a disease? How would I explain to my grandparents

Never Settle for Less

if I become pregnant? But Val demanded that I "woman up and stand on my own two feet." When you don't know how valuable you are, you will settle for anything.

"Okay, okay, please just leave me alone."

"Well, I'll be here if you need me. Have fun and tell me all the details," Val replied.

My legs were shaking and the palms of my hands were filled with sweat; I was so nervous.

"Kesha, are you ready to go out?" Allen whispered in my ear.

"Yes, I guess so. Where are we going?"

"Well there was a change in plans. I left my money at home so we can go to my house instead and eat some leftovers my mom made last night for dinner."

"Leftovers! Are you crazy? I don't eat leftovers. You said you were going to take me to the pizza shop. I'm going home. I will see you later." I turned and started to walk away.

"Okay, okay, Kesha. Just walk me home, and I can run into the house to get my money. Please."

"Well okay, but you better make it fast because my grandma will come looking for me if I'm not home at a certain time."

While walking with Allen to his house all I could hear was my grandma's voice saying, "a hard head makes a soft bottom."

How can I get out of this one? I asked myself. I knew something was going to happen. I knew he wanted more than pizza and maybe a kiss.

We arrived at his house, and no one was home. I was so nervous. He asked if I wanted to come inside, and I told him I'd just wait on the sidewalk.

"Kesha, it's okay. I won't hurt you; trust me." He looked at me with those beautiful eyes.

"Well, okay. I'll sit in the living room and wait for you."

He headed upstairs, and a minute later he called down, "Hey Kesha, you want to see something funny? Come up here and I'll show you something in my room from when I was a baby."

"No, I'm okay."

"Just come here," he said, with impatience in his voice. "I promise I won't hurt you or touch you."

"Okay, okay." I walked upstairs to his room. He showed me his baby picture.

"Aw, Allen, you were so cute when you were a baby."

"Yeah, I was a handful."

He grabbed me in an embrace and kissed me on my cheek.

"What in the HELL are you doing? Allen, get your hands off of me before I call the police."

"Call the police on me in my own house?"

"Yes, that's what I said. I am going to call the police on you and tell them you are trying to rape me."

"Rape! You, girl, are crazy. All I want to do is to get to know you better. That's all. I want to get closer to you. We have a lot in common, so don't be afraid. I know this is your first time having sex, but I promise I won't hurt you."

"Allen, please don't take this the wrong way, but I don't know you at all, and we don't have a lot in common. I hardly know you. I'm not about to have sex with you. I'm not ready for sex. We are only kids."

"Kids! Girl, I'm a man. What you talking about?"

"Whatever you are, I'm not having sex with you, so walk me back to school and I'll go home from there."

"I'm not walking you nowhere. Find your own way back home from here. I can't believe I wasted my time with you! If you want to be a virgin all your life, then you go ahead, stupid. Your girls ain't virgins. They grown women, so why you acting all stuck up like someone is going to hurt you?"

"Allen, I'm not ready to have sex with you. I'm just not ready!"

"Then get out of my house and walk home."

I left with tears in my eyes and walked home, hoping that none of my aunts or uncles would see me. If they did I would be in a world of trouble. Tears flooded my eyes so badly I had to stop walking to wipe them away. I couldn't believe that all he wanted from me was sex. Wasn't I worth more? This boy tricked me into believing his lies, and all he wanted was to get into my pants.

I felt ashamed, but relieved at the same time. If I had slept with him I would have been the talk of the school, the girl who had a one-night stand with Allen Tucker. And I couldn't have borne the shame of people laughing at me and other boys wanting to get with me just for sex. Did I mess up a good thing by not having sex with Allen? Only time would tell.

❧❧❧

"Hey, Mom, I'm home."

Grandma was sitting in her rocking chair, waiting for me to come through the door. She turned around, took one look at me, and said, "Whatever you planned on doing, it didn't work out, did it?"

"Grandma, what are you talking about?"

"You know exactly what I'm talking about. You never give what's precious to dogs because they will mistreat you every time."

I burst into tears. I told my grandma I was sorry. I didn't want to hurt her, but I explained to her I didn't know how to just be myself because the kids would make fun of me because I was still a virgin.

"You can't please everybody, Baby, and regardless of what you do, people are still going to talk about you, whether it be good or bad. Just appreciate who God created you to be. It's okay to be a virgin, Baby, because once you open that door and he enters in, you can't shut it."

Her words were encouraging and powerful, but hard to accept. She didn't know some of the things the other girls said at school about being a virgin. Peer pressure was all around me, and at times it felt easier to just give in. *God, please help me to know who I am and accept what you made me to be so I won't destroy my life before it even gets started,* I spoke softly in my heart.

"When you are in tune with God, He will show you what's a lie and what's the truth," Grandma said. "My walk with God is real, Baby, and I am always praying for my life and my family, especially you. God will give you what you need to be strong, Kesha, you just have to pray and ask. But in the meantime I am going to teach you how to pray and seek God for yourself because it's going to help you to accept who you really are on the inside when I'm long gone from this world."

I didn't understand what she was saying at the time, but with time and maturity I grew to understand. When you are in constant communion with God, He will show you the truth about yourself and about others. Grandma was right. Being honest with myself about how I felt toward myself was my first step toward accepting responsibility for my actions, and that was the next step toward maturity.

My grandmother knew I had told her a lie, and she allowed me to go anyway. She later told me that she had to teach me a lesson, but at the same time she forgave me.

"I see and know everything that's going on around me,"

she said. "I know more than I say, and notice more than you realize. I prayed for you this morning that God would keep you safe and protect you, and He did just that."

As a young child filled with insecurity, doubt, and many frustrations, I was a sitting target for many men who preyed on girls like me. I was young, beautiful, and still a virgin—and I suffered from low self-esteem. I thank God for a praying grandmother. God kept me from being hurt that day by someone who just wanted to use me.

The next day at school, Val ran up to me insisting that I tell her everything that happened between me and Allen.

"Nothing happened, Val. Nothing at all. As a matter of fact. I could not wait until the so-called date was over."

You should have seen the look on Val's face. She was astonished.

"Kesha, you mean to tell me nothing happened between you and Allen? So you used up a good lie for nothing?"

"Yes. I used up a good lie for nothing, and yes, nothing happened between me and Allen. All he wanted was to have sex with me, and I'm too young for that, and besides he's not my type."

"Kesha, you are one crazy girl. What do you mean he's not your type? Allen is every girl's type!"

I turned my head to look the other way, and Allen walked through the door. He had a big grin on his face and next to him walked Tameka Jones.

"Yo, Kesha, this could have been you, but you was too scared to give it up," he shouted across the lunchroom. All of his friends started laughing at me and calling out, "Yo, Kesha, you still a virgin?" "Y'all, she never got laid before."

Everyone was laughing and pointing fingers at me. All I could do was cry. I was so embarrassed I ran from the lunchroom to find a corner to hide in, but there was none. I could hear Val's footsteps behind me as she shouted, "Kesha! Kesha! Girl, hold up. It's going to be okay. We will get him back for saying that to you. I promise."

My eyes were overflowing with tears as I used the tail of my gym shirt to dry my face. Val tried to console me with kind words, but I was too hurt to hear them. Did I do the right thing? I asked myself over and over again.

I tried not to second-guess myself about my decision not to sleep with Allen, and after a few weeks I realized I had been right. His words, and the way he made fun of me in front of the entire school, proved to me I had made the right decision. Even Val realized I was right.

"I wish I'd had the courage to say no on my first date, but I didn't," she confided to me later. "I let others talk me into something I wasn't ready for. You did the right thing, and I'm happy for you. I'm sorry for trying to talk you into doing something you were not ready for."

Matthew 26:41: Keep alert and pray. Otherwise temptation will overpower you. For though the spirit is willing enough, the flesh is weak!

8. Friendly conversations

All he wants is power and control.

It was the end of the school year, heading into the summer break, and everyone was anxious to have fun, sleep in late, and waste the night away. Boy was I ready to enjoy my summer break with my friends before I would enter the "Big Leagues"—high school. Just the thought of the words sent chills through my body. I had to be prepared mentally and physically, and that meant I had to get my wardrobe together and my mind right. High school was stomping with the big dogs. I had to be on my A game or take the risk of being teased and bullied.

Every morning that summer my friends and I would meet in each other's yards or in Faircrest Park where we watched the boys play basketball. We would laugh, play around, crack jokes on each other, call the boys' names out, and run past with our jerry curls, white tennis shoes, and short jean shorts—boy were those the days. We were filled with so much energy. We were still kids.

One particular day I was in the park alone; the sun was beaming and the sweat was pouring down my back. I was on the swings thinking about how good summer felt. I was wondering if my friend Mark was going to be in the park shooting hoops. To my disappointment, he didn't show up. As I gave up the wait and headed home, I heard a voice.

"Hey, pretty girl, what's your name?"

"Who, me?"

"Yes, you. What's your name?"

"My name is Kesha. Why?"

"Because I couldn't help but take notice of you."

"So, you stalking me?"

"No, I just wanted to know your name."

Oh my god, this boy is so fine. How have I missed seeing him in the park? I was mesmerized. I thought I was going to melt like a piece of chocolate candy and drip all over the swings. I was so entranced I didn't even hear my grandmother calling.

"Kesha, get yourself home right now!"

When I finally heard her I was so embarrassed all I could do was put my head down and slowly walk away. As I looked back to say goodbye, he smiled. "You're a mama's girl. I understand. Go and listen to her, and I'll see you around the park some other time."

My grandma had headed over to the park and heard these last sentences. "You won't be meeting Kesha nowhere. You stay away from her, you hear? She will not be seeing nobody in no park because she's on punishment for the rest of the week."

I wanted to melt into the swings again, but this time from embarrassment.

"Yes, ma'am, I understand," he said, but then I grinned at him and said softly, so my grandmother wouldn't hear, "I will see you tomorrow." He smiled and shook his head. "Listen to your grandma. I'll see you another time if it's meant to be."

Is this boy for real? Here he is giving me a lecture about listening to my grandma. What was wrong with him?

He seemed so respectful and well-mannered; I knew my grandma would like that. When I got home Grandma gave me the whole lecture on listening and following directions. "Kesha, that boy is going to get you into a lot of trouble, so you better not see him ever again because all he wants is power and control."

"Oh my goodness, do you think every boy I meet wants only one thing, Mom?" I asked, shaking my head as I walked away. Grandma could be so annoying sometimes.

Throughout the night I tossed and turned. I could not sleep, thinking about what grandma had said. *Where does she come up with such words? Why is she so overprotective? I'm never going to have a life of my own, all I want is the freedom to do what I want. I know how to protect myself and act responsible.* Butterflies were forming in my stomach; I couldn't wait to see this boy the next day. I was so anxious and excited I practiced what I was going to say and thought about what I was going to wear until the wee hours of the morning.

༄༅

"Kesha," my grandmother yelled upstairs, "Get up; are you going to sleep your life away?"

"I don't have to go to school; please let me sleep," I called as I got up to use the bathroom. I looked at my clock, and it was 1:00 p.m.

"Oh my god, Grandma," I called, rushing down the stairs. Why did you let me sleep this late?"

"I told you to get up. You are on punishment."

"Punishment! For what?"

"Because you didn't come home when I called you, so

you are on punishment for a week. You are not to go off this porch. If your friends want to see you, then they have to come inside the yard."

"Oh, okay, Mom," I said, adding silently to myself that I would take this punishment any day. But something soon happened that changed that day for me. Grandma was going to the grocery store and that meant my Grandfather was going to drive her, because Grandma didn't drive.

Free at last! Free at last! Thank God, I was free at last! Nobody was home; I could do what I wanted to do.

I ran up the steps so fast that I missed a step and bruised my knees, but I didn't care. As soon as I heard the car pull off, I jumped into the shower, got my clothes on, and ran to the park. Guess who was playing basketball with the other boys? "Green eyes," the nickname I called him since I didn't know his name.

When he saw me he stopped playing basketball and came toward me.

"What's up? I thought you were on punishment the way your grandma came through this park yesterday."

"Well I'm not, so what's up with you? I don't have a lot of time to talk because my grandmother went grocery shopping and I have to be at the house when she comes back home."

"So you're Kesha. I'm Shawn."

"Do you live around here?" I asked,

"Yeah, I live around the corner from Greenwood Avenue with my sister."

"How old are you?"

"I'm 16. Is that too old for you?"

"No," I replied. I just like to know because my grandparents are very strict about who I meet and talk to."

"So when can I come around your house and meet your

grandparents?"

"I don't know about you coming to my house; my grandma don't care for you."

"She don't even know me."

"Well in her mind she already does."

"Oh well, that's how grandmas are about their grandchildren—overprotective. I'm going to come around anyway to meet your grandparents. Trust me, they'll like me."

We were so busy talking, I completely forgot about the time. When I did remember, I ran so fast through the park to make it home before my granddaddy's black long Cadillac turned the corner.

Beep, beep! Daddy was blowing his horn for me to come out and help with the grocery bags. As I walked toward the car, Grandma looked at me from the corner of her eye as if she knew I had been outside doing something I wasn't supposed to be doing.

"What, Mom? What did I do now?" I asked.

"Why? Are you guilty of something?"

"No."

"Well get these grocery bags and put them in the house."

The next day I was in the house watching my favorite TV show, *What's Happening Now*, when a voice in my front yard called my name.

I jumped out of my chair and ran to the front door, and there was Shawn outside talking to my grandparents. They were laughing and talking up a storm. What could Shawn be saying to them that was making them laugh like that?

"Kesha, come outside for a minute. Someone is here to see you."

As I walked to the door all I could see was Shawn smiling from ear to ear and those big green eyes looking at the door to see when I was going to come out.

"Hey Shawn, what's up?"

"How you doing?" Shawn replied. "I just came by here to see you for a minute while I was in the neighborhood."

I smiled every time he opened his mouth. He sounded so good and looked so handsome.

"Well, Shawn, Kesha won't be dating any boys right now because she has school to worry about. Do you go to school?" Grandma asked.

"Yes, Mrs. Williams, I do."

"Well where, son?"

Shawn paused and said hesitantly, "Trenton High."

"Then you understand how education is so important. I want nothing but the best for Kesha."

"I understand, Mrs. Williams. Kesha, I'll see you later. All right, Mr. and Mrs. Williams?"

Had Shawn gotten their permission to date me, without them ever seeming to realize it? Only time would tell.

Matthew 10:16: Look, I am sending you out as sheep among wolves. Be as wary as snakes and as harmless as doves.

9. Let the game begin

*Sometimes we have no clue
how hurtful a thoughtless word can be.*

The first day of high school and things were crazy; there were kids everywhere, looking for their classrooms, trying to get registered for classes, or trying to get their classes switched. You'd have thought they were giving away a prize—a really big prize, like a car or something. Everywhere I turned there were long lines, crowded hallways, kids and their parents standing around waiting for someone to assist them and direct them. Security guards made sure the lines were kept in order, zooming in and out to see if a fight was about to break out. Everyone around me was anxious and nervous, but also eager to find out what high school was all about.

Loud talking, conversations sparking from afar, yelling down the hallways, girls running with excitement to embrace their friends with hugs and kisses, parents talking about the conditions at the school or the teacher to student ratio, boys running to give their homeboys hand pounds: This was high school. I was nervous, not just about the new school, but about the way the other students looked, like they were grown adults. I couldn't tell the difference sometimes between the faculty, security guards, and students.

Oh god, I need to get out of this place. This is not the school for me. I need to be at another school that's way smaller than this one. I wanted to go home and tell Grandma to switch me to a different high school right away. But I managed to stay, and by the end of the day I'd embraced Trenton Central High School as my new home.

Every day seemed to get better. I learned how to read my schedule and find my classes. There were moments filled with fear, hope, and sadness. Self-determination was there but sometimes it seemed too far for me to reach. Every day after school I would go straight home and tell my grandmother all about my day. Some were better than others, of course. Every hallway I turned down I seemed to see a girl with a big belly. It was obvious a lot of kids were having sex and not using protection. Hallway A was Fashion Central; everyone would stand outside their lockers to see who had on the latest gear and kicks, boys waited for girls to pass by in tight jeans and fitted shirts and ask for their telephone numbers.

"Kesha, Kesha, is that you?"

I slowly turned to see who was calling my name.

"Girl, it's me, remember me? Lisa from Washington School. I was in your sixth grade class, remember?"

"Oh my goodness, Lisa. How are you doing, girl?"

"I'm doing fine. So how do you like it so far?"

"Well, it's okay I guess. I'm just trying to figure out some of the changes they made to my schedule."

"It's a learning process. Hey, do you want to cut this next class to go to the pizza shop across the street?"

"Are you serious? I'm trying to stay out of trouble, plus

NEVER SETTLE FOR LESS

you never know where my grandparents are going to be."

"Well I guess I'll see you later," Lisa said as she headed to the door.

I couldn't believe I had just been asked to cut class and it was only the third week of school. I had been tempted to say yes, but I could not afford to get into any trouble. And a good thing, too, because before I could step into my history class, I heard my name over the intercom, "Kesha Williams, please report to the main office."

Oh my god, what did I do? Had someone heard Lisa asking me to cut class with her?

As I slowly walked down the hallway and turned the corner I saw the principal, Mr. Raymond, dressed in a black suit. He was a short, round man, only about five feet, four inches, but with his walkie-talkie in his hand. I thought he looked mean walking toward me.

"Hi, young lady, how are you today?" he said, and although his tone was friendly, I was still suspicious.

"I'm okay," I replied cautiously.

"Do you have a pass to be in this hallway after the bell has rung?"

"Yes, I mean no, but I'm going straight to the main office because they called my name over the intercom."

"Okay, make sure you go straight into that main office, young lady."

"Yes, sir," I replied, and I noticed that as I slowly walked away he watched to make sure I did go to the office.

Once there I was told my guidance counselor wanted to see me, and to sit down and wait. I was nervous. I didn't understand why she had to go over my schedule again. It wasn't long before I figured it out.

"I'm Mrs. Davis, your guidance counselor. So if you have any questions or concerns about your schedule, or anything else, please stop by my office anytime," the counselor said as she led me to her office. Once seated I learned that my math and English classes were going to be changed. They had put me in the wrong class.

"What's wrong with the classes that I'm already in?" I asked anxiously. I liked my classes. I liked the new friends I was making in them.

"According to your IEP (Individualized Educational Plan), you should be in remedial math and English."

Oh, no not those words again!

"Remedial classes again!"

"Kesha, don't worry. They are to help you. Remedial classes are designed to help students who have problems understanding the basics concepts of a subject. It doesn't mean you are any less smart than the other students; you just need a little extra help."

"Okay, I understand," I said. I should have been used to hearing those words by now, but I hadn't wanted IEPs and remedial classes to be a part of my life in high school. But the sadness was tinged with relief. It was only a few weeks into the school year and I was already struggling in math and English. I didn't understand any of the material, and the teacher didn't have the time to sit with me to go over the lessons because she had so many kids in the class. I swallowed my pride; I had enjoyed being put in the regular classes, but I knew I needed the extra help.

"You'll see, Kesha," Mrs. Davis said with an understanding smile. "The classes are much smaller and the teachers are great. And it is only English and math; your other classes aren't changing."

Leaving Mrs. Davis' office I felt as if a ton of bricks had fallen off my back. I had my new schedule and I was ready to start fresh the next morning.

Never Settle for Less

I was happy to tell my grandma about the change when I got home. She was getting supper ready, and I noticed she didn't look so good.

"Grandma, are you sure you don't need to go to the hospital?" She hadn't felt well all day.

She said, "If I get worse I will go."

She slowly walked to the kitchen holding her stomach. *Oh God, what's wrong with my grandma? Please help her feel better.* I had never seen either of my grandparents sick; they were strong inside and out.

The next thing Grandma did made me even more worried. "Sit down for a minute and let me talk to you," she said. "Kesha, I'm not always going to be here to give you advice on what you should do. You are becoming a young lady, so it's time for you to grow up and start doing what leads to right living."

I didn't want to hear it. I rolled my eyes. *What is Grandma talking about? She acts like she is dying soon or something.*

"I raised you right, so don't disappoint me. Promise me that you will finish school and make something of yourself and not follow the rest of the crowd."

"Yes, Mom, I will, I promise I will make you proud of me, you and Granddaddy both."

I didn't want to hear Grandma's words that day, but I knew what she meant. Her words spoke loud and clear, like pure wisdom from above, but I wasn't in a place to receive what she was saying. God would never take Grandma away. He knew how much I needed her.

The next day I was up and ready to start my day right, anxiously waiting to meet my new teachers, fast-walking down the hallways trying to get to class on time before I was marked late. But for the life of me I couldn't find my classes.

Kesha Cox

Did the room numbers even exist? I paced up and down the hallways. Finally, a security guard told me I was in the wrong building. I needed to go to the C building.

"You don't look like you should be taking classes on that side of the building," he said as he walked away, leaving me confused.

When I arrived in the classroom there was only one other student there, sitting with his head on the desk.

"Come on in and have a seat," the teacher said. "I'm Mrs. Sandy, sit anywhere you like. I hope you are a student who wants to learn something, because I don't have time to waste on nonsense."

"Yes, ma'am, I do want to learn," I replied.

She gave me some test questions to check what level I was at, and as I finished them twenty minutes later, another student walked in. No book bag, no pencil, no paper, nothing in her hand. She asked for a pass to go back to her locker to get her books.

"No!" Mrs. Sandy said. "You come into this classroom late every day, unprepared. You will receive a zero for today. Kesha, look at this example before you; if you choose to come to my classroom unprepared, you will fail."

At the end of the period the bell rang, and as I approached the door I heard other students coming from other classes shouting down the hallway, "Look at the Special Ed kids."

I was so ashamed. I put my head down and rushed to my next class so nobody would see me leave that side of the building.

Too late! "Hey Kesha, hold up," I heard a voice shout. My friend Brian asked, "What are you doing coming from the C building? That's for the special kids. Do you have classes with them?"

NEVER SETTLE FOR LESS

"No way. I was just helping a teacher out with a project."

"Good, because I was about to say you don't look dumb."

I couldn't believe he had said that.

Children, teens especially, have no clue how hurtful a thoughtless word can be. I was so hurt and disappointed by his words. Would I ever get the chance to show that I wasn't dumb? I just needed extra help and support in my studies.

Psalm 141:3: Take control of what I say, Oh Lord, and keep my lips sealed.

10. Looks can be deceiving

Maybe I could help him, maybe I could change his mind about being in the streets, maybe I could help him desire better for himself.

After a long, challenging week of school, Friday arrived. It was a day of no worries, spent planning for the weekend, anxiously looking at the clock, and waiting for three o'clock so I could rush out of the door to walk home with my friends. You could see and feel the energy and the excitement as the students ran down the hallways, avoiding their lockers and heading straight toward the exit doors with smiles on their faces as bright as the noonday sun.

"Thank God it's Friday," I screamed as my feet touched the sidewalk.

My friends called my name from every direction. "Kesha, we are over here. Hurry up, girl and let's go to the store before we go home."

As we crossed the street I noticed a lot of boys standing in front of the store, flirting with every girl who walked by. "Oh god, here we go. Can we go to another store?"

"No, we can't," Tonya replied. "We are going to this

store. Who cares what these knuckleheads say or think about us?" Tonya was always the strong one in the group. She didn't take any mess from anybody.

As we approached the store all I heard was, "Yo, what's up?" "What's your name?" "Can I get those digits?"

I tried my best to quickly walk past them so I wouldn't be noticed. But Tonya had to stop and get her flirt on with one particular boy.

"Come on, let's go. I need to be home."

"Kesha, stop with the whining," she scolded. "Today is Friday; chill out, it's going to be okay. Don't your grandparents know you have a life of your own?"

I nervously paced back and forth waiting for her. These boys scared me. They looked rough. They had bags underneath their eyes, pants hanging below their waist exposing their underwear, hair not combed, tattoos on both arms, and the smell of marijuana reeking from their clothing. They looked like they had no regard for life, and at any moment a war could break out if you said the wrong thing to them.

"Tonya, I'll see you later. I'm going home. I don't have time to wait for you. I have somewhere to be," I said as I quickly walked away. I decided to walk straight up Greenwood Avenue where I could be seen if anything happened to me.

As I walked away with my head down, furious and upset with Tonya for wasting my time, I heard "Yo! Yo, Kesha!" At first I thought it was one of the girls calling my name, so I kept walking.

"Kesha, hold up." I heard my name again. I turned around and saw hands in the air, waving from side to side. As I walked closer I could see it was a boy, but I didn't know who it was. Finally, I realized that it was Shawn. I silently screamed, while trying to look cool on the outside. I hadn't seen him in months. He started running toward me as I smiled from cheek to cheek.

"Hey Kesha, I thought that was you walking from the store. How you been?"

"I haven't seen you in months since you were at my house."

"Well, allow me to give you a hug, if I may." Shawn was so polite, gentle, and respectful to me. Not like the boys in front of the store. And wow! Smooth caramel skin, a body that was toned and fit, and eyes that could light up the sky. I couldn't stop looking at him. He even smelled good. *Oh my god, if this is a dream I don't want to wake up.* He hugged me and I didn't want to let go; it was so easy to give in to whatever he wanted. I felt safe in his arms; his skin was soft and I inhaled a whiff of Egyptian musk oil.

"Shawn, you smell so good," I said.

"Thanks, and you look pretty today. Can I walk you home?"

"YES! Yes, you can walk me home."

He took my backpack off my shoulders and asked how my grandparents were doing. The difference between Shawn and those other boys couldn't have been clearer. He was a gentleman. He showed me respect. It was exactly what my grandmother had told me I should look for.

From that day on Shawn made sure I got home safe from school. He would wait for me outside the main doors. He never skipped a beat: Sunshine, rain, or snow, Shawn was right there, waiting patiently. We would walk to the pizza shop or the Chinese place to get something to eat and he would always suggest I get my grandparents something to eat so my grandma wouldn't have to cook. He was the perfect guy, and we hit it off so well. Could he be the one for me? My grandparents liked him; they thought he was a gentlemen, so respectful and so kind. They allowed me to go out to eat with him after school; they even allowed him to come into the house as long as we stayed in the living room where they could see us. Somehow he won their hearts over; they trusted him with me. I felt so safe with him. I felt as if no one or nothing was able to harm me.

"Shawn, I need to ask you a question. Why aren't you enrolled in school?" I asked one day.

"School's not for me. It's for people like you, because you're smart. Besides I'm too old, I'm 17. I would be a better fit for night school."

"Shawn, it's never too late to go back to school to get your education. Don't be so quick to give up on yourself."

Shawn smiled. "See, that's why I like you so much. You are a sweet person, and so encouraging. This is why I feel I have to protect you, because boys will see your sweetness and kindness and take it for granted."

Since Shawn had been walking me home every day and we were spending time together, Tonya felt that he had taken her place as my best friend. I would try and convince her that he hadn't, but she didn't believe me. She stopped talking to me, and so did the rest of the girls. They felt I didn't have time for them, and they were right because everywhere I turned Shawn was there.

I felt bad about it; one day I suggested to Shawn that he not meet me after school every day so I could walk home with the girls and spend some time with them. He became very upset with me. This was not the Shawn I was used to seeing. "Why are you worried about what your friends think? They are nobodies. They need to find other friends to walk home with. They are jealous over our relationship, Kesha, don't you see that?"

I saw I had hurt his feelings, so I apologized. I didn't want to see him upset or hurt. I didn't know how to explain to him that I needed a little space. I loved the attention and affection he showed me, but every day was a little too much. I wanted to make everyone happy: Shawn, Tonya and the rest of my friends. But how? How could I make everybody happy without hurting somebody's feelings?

ಸಂಬ

"Mom, I really need to talk with you about something."

"You're not pregnant, are you?"

"No, Mom!" I shouted "Why would you ask that?"

"Because you are getting older and I know having sex has crossed your mind a few times, especially with Shawn giving you all this attention."

"Well, Mom, that's not what I want to talk to you about. It's Shawn and everybody else at school. Some of my friends think Shawn is getting all my attention and I'm not spending time with them."

"Well, are you?" Grandma asked.

"Yes, but I don't know how to tell Shawn to give me some space without him feeling I don't want to be around him or hurt him."

"Well, how about I tell him for you? I'm tired of seeing his face around here every day anyway."

I smiled at Grandma. She always had a sense of humor. "Okay, but I thought you liked him."

"I do, but I don't need to see him every day," she laughed.

"Okay, then you can tell him, and this way I can walk home with the girls after school tomorrow. I do miss being around them."

"Always remember, you can't make everybody happy, Baby."

Never Settle for Less

My heart was in the right place, but often I would ignore how I really felt in order to make someone else happy.

The next day found me searching for my girlfriends. "Lynn, Lynn!" I shouted down the hallway. "What are you doing after school?"

"Nothing, why?"

"Well today we can walk home together if that's okay with you."

"Are you sure it's okay with Shawn?"

"Yes, trust me, it's okay."

But as soon as the bell rang the first person I noticed at the door was Shawn, laughing and talking with his friends.

"Hey Kesha," he said to me, and "I'll see you later," he added to his friends, "I have to walk my girl home."

"Shawn, I'm fine. I'm walking with Lynn today. You can go back and talk with your friends."

His face he turned completely red. I thought horns were going to come out of his head and smoke from his nose. He stood there simmering and didn't say a word. Lynn noticed, too.

"Kesha, it's okay. Let him walk you home before he has a cow."

"No, Lynn, I'm walking with you."

Shawn continued to stand there with a dead stare in his eyes as we walked away. I turned around, and he was still standing there with his hands in his pockets watching me.

He is crazy, I thought.

As we headed home Lynn asked me if I'd had sex with Shawn yet.

"No, what are you talking about?" But I knew exactly what she was talking about.

"No boy acts crazy like that unless you had sex with him. He acts like he can't stand to be away from you, he acts like he owns you. Every time we are together or you are with someone else he acts like he doesn't want them around you. Doesn't that worry you?"

"No, because he doesn't own me. My grandma told him I'm not going to be walking home with him every day. He's just going to have to accept that."

"Yeah, well I got a funny feeling about him, girl. Just be careful," Lynn replied.

I thought about Lynn's words and the fact that I didn't know everything about Shawn. Yes, he always wanted to be around me. What was wrong with that? Plus, I liked the attention he was giving me.

Later that day I heard my grandmother calling. "Kesha, come downstairs, Shawn is here."

What? I thought, *he didn't call and ask to come over.* As I fixed my clothes and put on my shoes my phone was ringing. It was my father calling to see how I was doing. My eyes lit up. I was as excited as if he had just walked through the door. We talked for a while and I forgot Shawn was downstairs. "Kesha," Grandma yelled. "Are you coming downstairs?"

"Yes, but I'm talking to my dad."

My dad heard everything in the background and suggested I go and enjoy my company. I ran downstairs and saw Shawn sitting in the living room with his hands folded and a look on his face as if he wanted to set me in order.

"Hey Shawn, what's up with you?"

Complete silence.

"Hello, I just said what's up with you?"

"Oh I'm sorry, I was daydreaming about something. Who were you on the phone with?"

"Excuse me?"

"Who were you talking to on the phone?" he said with

an edge to his voice.

"It was my dad, why?"

"Oh, okay, because I was waiting for you to come downstairs, and I've been waiting for some time now."

"Yes, but when my father calls everything that I'm doing stops."

"So he's more important than me?" Shawn asked.

"Yes! That's my father, Shawn!"

I could tell he didn't like my response. He didn't even blink his eyes. *This boy is a little off his rockers*, I thought, and for the first time I considered calling the relationship off. I decided I needed to talk with him about the changes I'd noticed in him, but when I mentioned how I felt, that he didn't want me to ever be around anyone but him, he told me I was wrong.

"Of course you can have whoever you want around you. I don't own you. We're just friends, right?" he said sarcastically. "I just like to be around you because you're such a nice person. But I feel if this relationship is going to go any further, I should be the only one you're thinking about."

I was lost for words. Was something really wrong with this boy, or was it me?

The longer we talked, the more questions I had for Shawn. Where did he work? Did he even have a job? Because every time I saw him he was always dressed up and always had new sneakers. His answer, "I have a little side hustle." What was that? "My uncle has a cleaning service where he cleans office buildings and I work for him."

For the life of me I didn't believe what he was telling me, but I didn't have any proof he was doing otherwise. The more questions I asked, the more it seemed as if he had an answer to validate his wrong. The more Shawn spoke, the more my heart turned away from him. I knew I had my personal issues, but this relationship was a little too much for me. Him not being in school, having no goals or priorities, always hanging in the streets. My conclusion: This boy must be selling drugs. Maybe we should just be friends. "Your lifestyle is a little too much for me," I told him.

But he didn't want to hear it. "Kesha, I really like you and want to be with you, just give me a chance to prove myself," he begged. "I promise I will change and do better."

I was impressed with Shawn's words and his emotional response. Maybe I could help him, maybe I could change his mind about being in the streets, maybe I could help him desire better for himself. But what would my grandparents think if I told them Shawn was not the person they thought he was?

1 Samuel 16:7: But the Lord say to Samuel, "Don't judge by his appearance or height, for I have rejected him. The Lord doesn't see things the way you see them. People judge by outward appearances, but the Lord looks at the heart."

11. Watch out for traps

A person who won't admit there is a problem can't be helped.

Lynn was my friend and the person I could trust to talk to when I needed advice, and I certainly needed it now.

"Did you sleep with Shawn?" were the first words out of her mouth.

"Oh my god, no, I did not sleep with him! This is much more serious. I think he's lying to me about his life. He doesn't go to school, he's always hanging in the streets, and every time I see him he has new sneakers and clothes. But if he's out there doing wrong I'm sure I can help him to change. I can help him be a better person. I can encourage him to get a job and go back to school," I said earnestly.

But Lynn was a skeptic. "No offense, but you're not strong enough for someone like Shawn. He'll change you instead of you changing him. You're not his type. He needs someone who's not going to take any nonsense from him. He'll run all over you. You're too nice. Plus you know he's controlling, and I've heard you're not his only girl. If I was you I'd end this relationship before he hurts you."

KESHA COX

If words could kill dreams, Lynn's should have killed mine. But I wasn't ready to listen. I didn't believe Lynn. My first thought was typical for most girls when they hear an unpleasant truth about their boyfriends: Lynn must be jealous that I finally had someone who was paying attention to me. I was so upset that I didn't speak to her for weeks, even though I knew in my heart she was right.

I had to try to help Shawn become a better person, didn't I? Grandma always said people sometimes need others to lend them a helping hand. She also said, "A person who won't admit there is a problem can't be helped." If Shawn really wanted to be with me he would show me by changing.

Knowing what I already knew about Shawn I should have let this relationship go. I wasn't street smart like him or the rest of my girlfriends. They knew when game was being played, and they knew how far to take it. I didn't. Even if I knew someone was lying to me over and over, I always gave them the benefit of the doubt and hoped that if I treated them nicely, they would do the same to me. It's good to think the best of others—but you also need to learn from experience. Yes, everyone can change, but not everyone is willing to change. My heart told me to end my relationship; that I was settling for less than I truly deserved, but I wasn't ready to listen.

Days turned into months and Shawn and I were still going strong. So many times I wanted to break the relationship off, but I was afraid he would get mad and hurt me. He became very demanding and possessive. He wanted to know my every move. My girlfriends, who had once been there for me, were there no longer. He had run them off with his mean, selfish ways. My male friends no longer said hi in the hallways or stopped to talk at my locker. Shawn had threatened them if they said anything to me. What was I going to do?

☙☙

"Kesha, I need to speak with you about something after class," Mrs. Sandy said as the bell rang one afternoon. "Is everything okay at home?" she asked when I took a seat next to her desk.

"Yes, why do you ask?"

"Because I noticed you haven't been doing your homework like you used to. Your test scores are low this marking period. This is not like you. What's wrong, sweetie?"

"Oh nothing, Mrs. Sandy. I'm just a little distracted lately, that's all."

"Fine, but I need for you to get back on track. It's almost the end of the marking period and I would hate for you to take a bad grade home to your grandparents."

I knew exactly what Mrs. Sandy was talking about. I was too busy courting Shawn. He had all my attention, and I was so busy hanging out with him that I was forgetting the important things, like my schoolwork, spending time alone with myself, and hanging with my friends. I felt like I was in a marriage filled with commitment and responsibility, but still a kid looking to find her way. Oh my god, what would Grandma say?

James 1:5: If you need wisdom—if you want to know what God wants you to do—ask him, and he will gladly tell you. He will not find fault with your asking.

12. The C word

If you ever needed to talk to God, just open up your mouth and he will listen, and answer when he is ready.

When I got home that afternoon the house was quiet and no one was in sight. "Mommy, Daddy," I called out loud. It was not like them not to be home. I ran up the steps shouting and looking for my grandparents. The phone rang; it was my grandfather telling me Grandma had to be admitted in the hospital because she was sick. I stood there shaking as I asked what was wrong with her. "She'll be okay, I will be home shortly," he told me as I hung up the phone and fell to my knees to cry out to God, "Please, God, don't take my grandma away. I'm not ready for her to leave me. Please, whatever is going on in her body, please fix it. I need my grandma; she's all I got."

I ran out the front door and walked toward Hamilton Avenue where St. Francis Medical Center was located, crying all the way there.

When I arrived at the hospital, all I could think about was finding her room.

"Excuse me, sir," I spoke nervously to a gentleman

Never Settle for Less

behind the security desk. "I'm here to see my Grandma, Elizabeth Williams."

"When did she arrive here at the hospital?"

"Today; my grandfather told me they were here."

It took only seconds to look up Grandma's information, but it seemed like forever. The man at the desk gave me directions to her room, and I took off running to the nearest elevator.

There she was in the hospital bed, covered in layers of blankets; face pale, skin cold on some parts of her body and warm on others. A heart monitor was hooked up to her chest and an IV needle was in her arm. "Mommy," I whispered in her ear, "Are you okay?"

Her eyes opened slowly. "I will be as long as the good Lord allows," she smiled with tears rolling down her face.

"Mommy, please don't leave me. What can I do to make it better? Just say it. Why are you here, what's wrong? Please tell me so I can help you."

"Grandma is getting old, Baby. They said I have to start taking treatments."

"What kind of treatments, Mommy?"

"Chemotherapy, Baby. Grandma has breast cancer."

"Breast cancer?" I repeated nervously. "Grandma, what is that?"

"Baby, you wouldn't understand it."

She was too tired to say any more. She looked as if all the life was being drained out of her. I gently laid my head on her chest and quietly listened to her heartbeat. I thought about when I was a little girl and would have nightmares. She would come into my bedroom and I would lay my head on her chest and fall asleep. This day I listened to her heartbeat and prayed that God would heal my grandma so that she could come back home to her family.

KESHA COX

Grandma always said if you ever needed to talk to God, just open up your mouth and he will listen, and answer when he is ready. I knew there was a God, and I knew God lived in Grandma. I knew how to pray because my grandma had taught me, but I didn't know if God had heard my prayers for my grandma on that day. But, He did. He answered, and Grandma was released from the hospital two days later.

Psalm 145:18: The Lord is close to all who call on him, yes to all who call on him sincerely.

13. I SHOULD HAVE LISTENED

Never give what is precious to dogs; they will destroy what you give them every time.

It was a cold and windy Saturday; ice was hanging from the trees and from the rooftop. Cars were covered with ice, and the street looked like a sheet of glass. I stayed in the house with Grandma as she sat in her rocking chair covered in blankets. There was nothing more important than being with her; she needed me to care for her and nurse her back to health. The chemotherapy treatments took a lot out of her. Grandma was weak, she was fatigued, she had no appetite to eat, and she was slowly losing her hair. Daddy came busting through the door after putting rock salt down on the ground to melt the ice.

"Man, it's cold out there," he shouted as he walked through the house with his cigarette in his mouth and hat, gloves, and coat in his hands.

No matter what job he was doing, Daddy always had a cigarette in his mouth. His jackets were filled with holes because of his cigarettes. "Lil, how you feeling?" he asked my grandmother, as he headed to the kitchen to make some supper. He'd taken over the cooking, because she was too sick to do it.

"Daddy, do you want me to help you?"

"No way, I don't need no help. Besides you like to cook with that garlic salt and I don't like garlic in my food. You stay in there with your grandma," he said as the two of us laughed at him. Daddy was such the character; he had a way of making you laugh even when he was serious.

The phone rang, and when I answered, it was Shawn. He wanted me to go with him to meet some cousins. "I've been talking about you to them," he said. "Can you go with me to see them?"

I told him I'd planned to spend the day with my grandmother, taking care of her, but he insisted, saying it would only be for a short time. They lived in North Trenton, he told me, as I explained that my grandparents would never let me go that far without them.

"Just tell them that you are going to your friend's house down the street for a little while and meet me in the park. We can catch a cab out there."

What had happened to the boy who told me not to disobey my grandma? Now Shawn wanted me to lie to my grandparents. This wasn't like him; this fool was up to something. Something didn't feel right, but, still, I told him I'd meet him in an hour.

Nervous and scared because I didn't know what to expect from Shawn's family, I went to meet him in the park. He was waiting for me with a big smile that made me even more suspicious. I kept telling myself I should just stand up to him and go back home, but I knew he would get mad if I did. I hated to see him mad.

We walked to the train station to catch a cab, my first time ever. My grandfather always drove me anywhere I needed to go.

"I can't wait for you to meet them, they are going to love you," Shawn said with excitement. He was persistent in getting me to go to his cousin's house, but my heart was telling me this was something more. Shawn wanted to have sex as well. We'd been together for months, and I was sure it crossed his mind because it crossed mine, but I knew I was too young to be having sex. *"Okay, if I can tell Allen Tucker no, I can tell Shawn no, too!"* I thought.

When we got there I found we were in the middle of the projects. This only made things worse. I hadn't expected this. I thought they lived in a house.

"What? You never been in the projects before? Is this beneath you?" Shawn said angrily.

"It's okay if this is where your family lives," I said, but I'd always heard terrible stories about the projects. If my grandparents knew I was here they would have a cow. I would never be able to see daylight again! But I headed in beside Shawn.

When I walked in everyone was so kind. "We've heard so much about you," and "Now, how did a nice girl like you meet someone like my cousin?" Shawn shook his head at his cousin as if to say don't scare this girl. Shawn knew I was very timid, so he asked if I wanted to go into his cousin's bedroom to watch TV so we could have more privacy. "No!" I replied, remembering Allen. He persisted and went back and forth until I just gave in and went with him.

As soon as we were in the bedroom, Shawn insisted I close the door to give us some privacy, but I refused. What would his cousins think? But suddenly I heard the front door close and the house got quiet. Shawn closed the bedroom door, and even when I asked, he wouldn't open it.

He turned on the television and insisted that I sit on the

bed with him to watch. I just wanted to go home.

"Stop acting like a damn baby," he shouted, "You are getting on my nerves with this whining." He got up off the bed and started pacing the floor, his anger spilling out at me. "I'm trying to treat you nice and respectful, but you keep acting stupid."

I froze. I didn't know what he was about to do. His face was red and his fists were balled up. "Do you think I'm going to hurt you? Do you?" he persisted.

"No, Shawn, I'm just not ready to have sex."

"Kesha, we've been dating for months now and you're not ready. Stop playing with me. I promise I won't hurt you."

I was terrified. Shawn was turning into a madman before my eyes. I wanted to call my grandparents, but I couldn't. Shawn would never allow it. He wouldn't take no for an answer. I told him I was afraid of getting pregnant. I told him I was afraid because it was my first time. He had protection, he told me, and he'd take care of me. He calmed down a little and told me he loved me. "We have to take this relationship to the next level," he said, and I said fine—anything to keep him calm.

"See, my kisses are sweet. I love you, I promise you I won't hurt you," he said as he kissed my cheeks and my neck, holding me close. I could feel his heart beat; his lips were soft and tasted so sweet, and then it happened. We had sex. It wasn't very pleasant. It was my first time, but Shawn seemed like a pro, and he made my body feel comfortable; he calmed my fears and nervousness. He held me close to him as if he was a shield of protection.

"See," he said when it was all over. "I told you I wouldn't hurt you. Did I keep my promise?" I stared at him blankly. I couldn't believe I'd just given my virginity away.

"Are you alright?" he asked.

"Yes, I'm okay, I just feel bad about what just happened."

"Well who has to know besides me and you?" he asked, thinking this was a reasonable answer.

"Please take me home," I told him. I knew I had done wrong, but I was already making excuses to myself. I was under a lot of pressure. I didn't want Shawn to be mad at me. I didn't want him to leave me. So I gave in because I wanted to be with him and he said he loved me.

But what would my grandparents say if I told them? And somehow I was sure that my grandmother would know even if I didn't tell her. What would she do to me? How would she feel about me? "God, please forgive me," I prayed, "because I know what I just did was wrong."

Another voice inside me said, "Kesha, stop acting like a little girl. You are old enough to have sex, you're 15 years old. Grow up." But deep inside I wasn't old enough, I was just a child.

When I got home Grandma was sitting in her chair, still not feeling well, and Daddy was upstairs watching TV. I told her I needed to take a shower because I had helped Lori and her mom clean out the basement. The lies just kept flowing, always one more to cover the last one. If Grandma had known what was going on, she would have gained the strength of a lion and devoured me and Shawn.

The next day Shawn called to check on me, to see how I was doing. He said he was sorry for pressuring me into having sex. I told him I didn't want to talk and to call me back later, and soon after I heard the doorbell ring. Shawn was downstairs. He was talking with my grandmother about what she was going to plant in her garden in the spring. I quickly ran down the steps, I was sure he was going to tell my grandmother what had happened. I took him into the living room, away from my grandmother.

"Shawn, popping up at the house isn't good. Can you let me know next time you're coming over?"

It was the wrong thing to say. I was just worried he would tell my grandparents what we'd done, but he had other ideas.

"What? So are you expecting someone else to come over?" he asked angrily.

"No, I'm not, calm down." I said as he shouted and pointed his finger at me.

"Is everything okay in there?" Grandma shouted.

"Yes, Mom, everything is okay. Shawn, please stop talking to me that way. I don't like that."

But he didn't stop. "Well get yourself together! I'm leaving and I'll be back later, and hopefully you will be ready to talk."

My heart was pounding as if it was going to jump out of my chest. I needed to end this relationship, and soon!

Hours later Shawn returned, and though I answered the door, it was too late for me to have company. My grandparents were already upstairs asleep. Shawn stood with his foot in the middle of the doorway to keep me from closing it.

"We are going to talk now. What is your problem? Don't you want me anymore?" he questioned.

"Shawn, why are you acting crazy, as if I did something to you?"

"Let me in so we can talk."

"I can't; my grandparents are asleep."

"I need to talk to you now. I don't want to wait until tomorrow."

As usual, he wore me down and I let him in the house so he wouldn't get any more upset.

"Okay, so what do you want to talk about? It's 9:30 at night. If my grandparents knew you were here they would be so angry. You have to leave soon."

Now that he'd gotten me to let him in he seemed ready to leave. "Okay, give me a kiss goodbye," he told me. I kissed him; he held me close, kissing me on my neck and instantly I gave in.

ಬಿಲ್ಸ

Every time we were together, the more I gave in to him, the more aggressive, controlling, and demanding he became. He wanted things his way. I was so afraid of him: I was afraid to say hi to any of my friends, male or female. He thought I wanted any boy I spoke to. No one could walk home with me, not even my girlfriends. He was out of control. One day at school I was on my way to lunch, and one of my male friends wanted to walk with me. Out of nowhere Shawn came up and threatened him. I was so afraid I told Joe to go to lunch without me. How had Shawn gotten into the building? Somebody had to have let him in.

"If I catch you talking to him again, I'm going to show you how crazy I really am," he threatened, and knocked my books out my hand.

It never failed. Every time he did something crazy he made up later by buying me expensive jewelry, getting my hair done, or going shopping. Shawn was becoming a madman, but he still had his sweet side. A lot of people, like my grandparents, never saw crazy Shawn. They trusted him; they didn't know some of the things he was doing to me.

I had no one to talk to; no one had a clue about how Shawn was treating me. My grandmother was sick. She didn't need to hear my problems; she had problems of her own. My grandfather would kill him if he knew. I held in my anger, my hurt, my regrets, and my disappointment. This was not the life I wanted. Everything was falling apart, one puzzle piece at a time.

☙❦

It was quiet in the house; you couldn't hear a single thing. My grandparents were upstairs settling in for the night. "Kesha, don't be up too late, you have school tomorrow," Grandma called down. Shawn and I were watching TV, laughing and talking about the episode of *What's Happening Now* we had seen last week.

"Shawn, I need to talk to you about something, but I need your undivided attention so you can hear what I'm saying to you."

"Okay," he replied and turned off the TV.

"Shawn, it hurts me when you talk to me bad in front of my friends. I like you a lot, but if we are going to be together you need to change your ways."

He jumped up and punched me in the mouth so hard I fell to the carpet. Blood was everywhere: on the carpet, on my clothes. My lips were busted, top and bottom. I couldn't stop the bleeding. I was crying so hard Shawn covered my mouth so my grandparents wouldn't hear me. "Shut up before I hit you again. You had this coming, so don't start crying now to your grandma, you spoiled bitch."

"Shawn, please get away from me," I said, holding my lip, my hands filled with blood and my mouth burning. I wanted to run upstairs and tell my grandparents, but instead I ran to the kitchen to try and stop the bleeding. "My grandfather is going to kill you. Get out of my house now," I shouted.

"I'm not going anywhere," Shawn came toward me as if he was going to hit me again. I tried to run, and he grabbed me from behind and got in my face. "You don't listen to me. You never listen!" he shouted. "If you tell anybody it's going to get worse. I promise you."

He had no remorse as I stood there bloody, holding my lip. He gave me his dead stare. *This man is crazy, what did I get myself into, how can I end this relationship without him killing and ending my life? God, please help.*

I knew that Shawn was going to hit me again, this was just the beginning because I allowed him to get away with the first time.

Grandma always said never give what is precious to dogs; they will destroy what you give them every time.

Matthew 7:6: Don't give what is holy to unholy people. Don't give pearls to swine! They will trample the pearls, then turn and attack you.

14. Never settle for less

Love shouldn't hurt, nor does it beat the other person when it can't have its way.

I knew that Shawn was going to hit me again; it was just a matter of time. Accepting the first hit was an open door to many more. Being in a relationship with Shawn was like being in a nightmare. Was there a way to escape? I would often ask myself this, and the answer to my question was always no. He would kill me before letting me go. He had already made that known to me over several occasions. I was only fifteen years old and going through the worst experience of my life. This guy appeared nice, sweet, and kind when I first met him. I guess that was just to win me over—well, it worked! He said he loved me and wanted to be with me and protect me from the rest of the guys who would try and take advantage of me. If it was the truth at first, it turned out later to be a lie. He was doing to me what he didn't want others to do. I made excuses for every beating and every hit Shawn gave me because I felt both sorry for him and afraid of leaving him. I blamed his past for his behavior. He would say often that he couldn't control his

NEVER SETTLE FOR LESS

anger and if I would just listen the beatings would stop. He would see his father beat his mother every night when he was a child because she wouldn't listen to his father, so his father made her listen.

The morning after that hit I was in so much pain I could barely open my mouth. My eyes were puffy because I had cried so much the night before.

"Kesha, it's time to get up," Grandma shouted.

"Mom, please come here for a minute," I whispered softly.

"What is it, child?" Grandma asked as she came closer and saw my swollen lip. "Kesha, what happened to you? What's wrong with your lip?"

"Last night when I was trying to get a glass from the cabinet. I opened the door really fast, and hit my lip."

"Kesha, I don't believe you. I have seen you open those cabinets many times and that has never happened to you. Did Shawn hit you? You better tell me the truth. Did he hit you? I'm calling the police. Roscoe, get up these steps and look at this child's lip."

I was terrified. What would happen if she called the police? Shawn would kill me—and maybe my grandparents, too. "I hate being in this house, I hate everybody in here," I shouted out loud. I didn't mean anything I said. I was only angry at one person, and that was Shawn.

"Don't you talk to me like that, do you understand me?" Grandma shouted back, then pleaded. "Baby, just tell me the truth. Did Shawn do this to you?"

"No, Mom, please don't call the police, please. He didn't. I told you what happened. I have to get ready for school."

"No, you're not going to school like this; you can barely talk. You are staying home."

Kesha Cox

"Mom, I can't, please, I have to go to school."

I hurried and got dressed; I knew I was going to be late but I didn't care. I had to get to school because Shawn was going to be looking for me after school. This is how afraid I was of him.

"Kesha, do you need me to walk you to school?" Daddy asked.

"No, Daddy, I'm okay."

"If Shawn did this to you, you better tell us so we can call the police."

"Daddy, he didn't do it. I wouldn't lie to you and Mommy."

"You know your grandmother is sick and she can't deal with all this drama. I won't have this mess around my house."

"Okay, Daddy, I understand."

As I entered the school it seemed as if everybody knew about what Shawn had done to me. Everywhere I walked the other kids were looking and staring at me. I knew why; it was obvious because of my busted and swollen lip. As I entered my classroom everyone looked at me as if I were a ghost. Mrs. Jackson dropped her lesson book from her hand and said, "Kesha, come into the hallway so I can talk to you for a moment."

I told her my lie, but she didn't believe me.

"Who is this Shawn I keep hearing about from your friend Lynn?" she asked.

"Mrs. Jackson, he didn't do it."

"I never asked you if he did it. Did he do this to you?"

I nodded my head yes as tears fell from my eyes.

"Mrs. Jackson, please help me, I don't know what to do. I'm scared. I want out of this relationship but he won't let me out."

She suggested we go to the main office, talk to the principal, and call my grandparents. I was terrified. My grandparents would call the police.

"They should call the police," Mrs. Jackson replied. "No man should ever put their hands on a woman. Ever! You are no punching bag for anyone. You are too beautiful and too special for anyone to be putting their hands on you. Shawn needs a good whooping from your grandfather for what he did to you." Mrs. Jackson was so upset, she responded on my behalf as if I was her very own daughter in trouble.

I was so afraid that entire day; all I could think about was what Shawn had told me: If I wasn't ready when he came for me after school, he would show me what he was made of. He's going to kill me, for sure. All day I sat in the principal's office, being interviewed by the guidance counselors, the school nurse, and the police. They asked me all types of questions: Shawn's whereabouts, his place of residence, what he looked like. I felt a little safe while everyone was there, but what about when they all left? What would happen to me?

I gave the police a report of what happened the night before. I told them everything Shawn had said and done. Every security guard in the school was on high alert. Shawn was not allowed on school grounds or near me. My grandparents were called, and the police and principal explained that the next step was placing a restraining order on Shawn. At the end of the day Daddy was outside waiting for me to come out so he could drive me home.

"Thank you, Daddy. I'm sorry for putting you and Mommy through this."

Daddy was never the one to say much, but when he spoke he meant business.

"Kesha, I'm telling you right now, I better not ever see

Shawn around my house again and you better leave him alone or you will find yourself without a place to live."

Did Daddy mean what he said about putting me out of his house? I asked my grandma. She told me he was just disappointed in me and hurt because I allowed someone to hurt me. But both of them made it clear I was never to see Shawn again.

I went into my room and started to cry. I wished my father was there. He would have protected me from all of this pain. Shawn would have thought twice before putting his hands on me then.

When the phone rang I was scared to answer it because I knew it would be Shawn. Grandma marched into my bedroom and just turned the ringer off. "Kesha, I know I haven't been as active with you as I was before I was sick. The chemo takes a lot out of me, Baby, and I don't know if I will ever get better."

"Grandma, what are you saying? Why are you even taking this chemo?" I asked. I didn't understand anything about chemotherapy or what it was for—then.

"I have cancer, Baby. Breast cancer, like I told you, and they have to remove one of my breasts soon before the cancer spreads. I want you to know that Grandma ain't gonna be around always. I'm growing tired, Baby, but please promise me that you will finish school and make something of yourself. Please, Baby, promise me that you will."

"Yes, I promise, Mommy. I will not disappoint you."

Grandma decided it was time to have a serious talk about sex. When I confessed I had had sex with Shawn, all she said was, "Well, I wish you had waited, but did ya'll use any protection?"

She seemed reassured when I told we had used a condom.

"Kesha, there is so much more in the world for you to see and experience, and believe me, Shawn is not in your future. I'm glad you were smart enough to use some protection because you don't need any babies or these diseases that're running around here. One day you will understand that I am only trying to help you to make better choices for your life."

"I know, Mom," I said softly.

༺༻

The news about what Shawn had done to me got out; my family was concerned and furious. My uncles were ready to go find him. I hadn't heard from him in days. It was as if he had left the face of the earth. Everything was quiet at school, and at home the phone wasn't ringing off the hook. I had a lot of support from my teachers and even my girlfriends.

A few days later I heard Lynn shouting my name down the school hallway. Someone had seen Shawn somewhere in the building. My heart was beating so fast. I was scared. Shawn knew my schedule better than me, so he could wait for me anywhere in the building. And he did. I heard he had paid a security guard to come into the school so he could talk to me.

"Kesha," my heart seized in fear when I heard his voice, and fear paralyzed me and kept me from running. "Please forgive me for putting my hands on you. I miss you. I will do anything to be with you again, please, forgive me."

"Shawn, I can't. My grandparents will not allow me to see you again. It's over, and besides it will never work between me and you. We are two different people going in two different directions."

"No, Kesha you are wrong. We are meant for each other," he said despairingly.

Shawn was persistent. Every day he would send messages by one of his boys. The phone calls started again; he left messages saying he was sorry and pretending to cry. Finally, I felt sorry for him and gave in. When he asked to come over, I said yes.

I knew it was disobedient to see Shawn, but a part of me believed he was sorry for what he had done. When I opened the back door all I could see were balloons with "I love you" printed on them and a bright red bag in Shawn's hand. It wasn't even Valentine's Day. I was only fifteen. I fell for it.

"It's for you; this is how much I love you and want to be with you again. I'm sorry for what I did to you, I will never put my hands on you again," he promised.

My heart dropped to the floor. *He must be really sorry.*

"Shawn, this is beautiful," I said as I looked inside the bag and saw a lovely pair of earrings with my name in them. "They are beautiful. I love them. I have never received anything like this from anyone."

"I told you I love you. And I'm sorry for hitting you."

I forgave him. I let him come into the house without my grandparents knowing, and we made up. He was once again back in my life. My heart was saying no the entire time. Love shouldn't hurt nor does it beat the other person when it can't have its way. Settling for less than I deserved cost me a life of living free.

1 Corinthians 13:4-8: Love is patient and kind; love is not jealous or boastful or proud or rude. Love does not demand its own way. Love is not irritable, and it keeps no record of when it has been wronged. It is never glad about injustice but rejoices whenever the truth wins out. Love never gives up, never loses faith, is always hopeful and endures through every circumstance.

15. Grandma

I have no worries; God is going to see me through this.

One Saturday evening the family gathered around the house for a meeting concerning Grandma. It was nothing like having my aunts, uncles, and cousins over for the usual Saturday night family gathering when we would eat, watch movies, and play games while the adults would play cards. This Saturday, after eating, the family gathered around the living room so Grandma could announce that she had breast cancer. She told us the doctor had suggested she have one of her breasts removed so the cancer wouldn't spread to other parts of her body.

Some were shocked, others already knew about Grandma's condition. There were so many questions and concerns, Grandma was unable to answer all of them. She just said, "I have no worries. God is going to see me through this surgery, for He is the one who has the final say-so."

She believed the surgery was the best thing for her, and so did her doctor, Dr. Mack. As a family we prayed that God would grant her mercy to wake up, and the grace to heal.

Grandma constantly told me that she would be all right.

KESHA COX

She always had a way of calming one's fears; I felt peaceful after she spoke to me, but though there was peace, when I heard the news I ran upstairs to my bedroom and sat in my dark corner to cry. I felt Grandma was never going to come back home once she went to the hospital for that surgery.

The weekend passed, and I sat in school the entire day anxiously waiting to hear how Grandma's surgery had gone. Before my class ended I asked if I could go to the main office to make a phone call to check on her condition. Daddy answered the phone sounding happy and relieved. Everything had gone well, and Grandma was doing fine.

"Thank you, Jesus!" I yelled down at the main office. "My Grandma is coming home and we are going to beat this cancer!"

Everyone in the office looked at me like I was crazy, but I didn't let that stop me from rejoicing.

St. Francis Medical Center was around the corner from the school, so as soon as the bell rang I ran past my locker and straight out the doors so fast I almost ran the security guard over. I ran with excitement as the wind beat against my face, reminding me of a fresh start and the sense of freedom and relief for my grandma. I was anxious as I approached her room where she lay in the hospital bed with a smile on her face. I could tell she was sore and in pain.

"See, Kesha, I told you God was going to see me through this surgery. He's not finished making Grandma's wings yet. Now, help me do something with my hair," she smiled in pain.

Another burden was lifted from me as I played with her hair. This woman meant the world to me. God knew how much I needed her, and He had answered my prayers once again by allowing Grandma to go through her surgery successfully.

Never Settle for Less

Dr. Mack suggested she continue to take the chemotherapy at least once a week for a few months just to make sure there were no more cancer cells. The good news made everyone in the family happy. It made us all appreciate life the more. As she got better, every day Grandma would find different activities to do around the house and the yard to keep her mind at ease. She loved to be in her garden where she and my grandfather grew field peas, string beans, corn, and her favorite, okra. This was therapy for Grandma; she said it made her feel grateful to be alive to enjoy life, family, and the things that she loved to do the most. Her favorite line was, "Another day in the land of the living is another day filled with life." Grandma seemed stronger than ever, both mentally and physically. She was cooking, cleaning, and going up and down the stairs again as she had before she had gotten sick. Even a cold couldn't get her down; her mind was sharper than ever before.

"Kesha, come in here and help me put these greens in this ziplock bag. Let me ask you something, and I want you to be honest with me. Are you pregnant?"

"Pregnant! No way, Mom, what makes you say that?"

"Because I had a dream about fish and that means that someone in the family is pregnant."

"Well, Mom, it's not me. Having kids is far from my mind. Besides I'm just a kid myself."

"Speaking of lying, Kesha, you've been lying to me and your grandfather about seeing Shawn again."

"Mom, what are you talking about? I'm not seeing Shawn!" I'd become very good at lying.

"If you don't leave that boy alone, he is going hurt you really bad. You may beat me to the grave. A hard head makes a soft bottom, Kesha, you better listen."

I was shocked by Grandma's words. But she was on

point, and she always spoke the truth. If she only knew what I was really going through, it would probably cause her to become sick again. So I kept silent about Shawn.

Shawn couldn't keep a promise if his life depended on it. As soon as he got comfortable with being with me again he struck again. Walking to class with my friend Joe, Shawn appeared out of nowhere.

"I need to talk to you!" Shawn demanded.

Joe knew all about Shawn. "Kesha, I don't want to leave you alone with this dude. Are you going to be okay?" he asked.

I told him it would be all right. Surely Shawn wouldn't hit me right there in the school hallway.

"What did I tell you about talking to other dudes while I'm not around?" He started as soon as Joe walked away.

Suddenly the hall was very empty. Nobody was around, not even the security guards. As I turned the corner toward the C building, Shawn grabbed me by my shirt and slapped me across my face. I thought I was going to pass out; he hit me so hard. He forced me to leave school, saying if I screamed or made a noise he would hit me again. Pretending not to be in pain, holding back my tears, we walked to his sister's house. I hoped I would see someone I knew, but no one was around.

At his sister's house I was too afraid to say anything. His sister headed to the grocery store, telling us only to lock her door when we left. Could she not see that I was crying, the left side of my face swollen from Shawn's slap? As soon as we reached the top steps Shawn slapped me again and I fell to the floor, trying to cover my face as he kicked me all over my body. I pleaded with him to stop; I was in so much pain from his kicks. The door opened.

"Shawn, stop hitting her. Get off of her before I call the

cops myself!" his sister shouted.

He pushed his sister; they fought, and I ran next door where the neighbors called the police.

But before the police could get there I ran away. I never told Mommy and Daddy about it; I knew they would get upset.

Psalm 66:19: But God did listen! He paid attention to my prayer.

16. THE C WORD AGAIN

Your love for me was unconditional in every area of my life. You were grace and mercy before I knew the true meaning of it. You kept me even when I didn't want to be kept. Your love for me will never go unnoticed. You are the woman I wish and long to be.

A year after Grandma's surgery she became sick again, and nobody knew what was wrong with her. Some days she felt great, and other days she felt weak.

"Mom, are you okay?" I would ask her, and her answer would always be, "I'm okay, I just have a little cold."

But I knew it was more than a cold. Grandma was sick again with the cancer. It had come back, and she wasn't telling anybody. Or was she just not telling me?

One day Dr. Mack called. I happened to answer the phone. "Kesha, your grandmother is not doing well," he told me. "The cancer has come back and is continuing to spread. We are still giving her the chemo, hoping something will change for the better, but at this point there's really nothing we can do."

My heart dropped. "What do you mean there is nothing

you can do?"

"I'm sorry. If the chemo doesn't help, then there's not much after that we can do."

Grandma was once again in and out of the hospital, starting chemo all over again. Her body was weak and slowly wasting away day by day. She wouldn't eat anything; she was very fatigued and losing weight. She was losing her hair, and it seemed as if life was slowly leaving her body. Breathing became difficult, and she said that if she was going to die she would rather die at home with her family. My family respected her wishes. A hospital bed was brought in and weeks later hospice was called to make her comfortable.

Every night I would sleep in the bedroom with her, in her favorite rocking chair. An oxygen machine ran throughout the night making loud noises, and I could hear Grandma breathing hard as her eyes watered with tears.

"Mommy, it's going to be okay. I promise God is going to make you well because I prayed," I told her. She would barely smile. "God if anything happens to Grandma my life is over; I can't live without her," I prayed. But day after day her breathing got worse, and her body was slowly shutting down. Hospice nurses came to make sure she was comfortable. Her skin was breaking down very quickly; she began to get bed sores and rashes all over her body. My aunts would wipe away the sweat from her forehead and the drool away from her mouth. I knew Grandma wasn't going to make it; I just didn't know how to accept the fact that she was going to leave me very soon.

Friday, April 30, 1993, I woke with such a sadness in my heart. I ran down the hall to Grandma's room to see if she was still alive. She was. *Why do I feel this way? As if I lost my best friend? Grandma is still here.* Daddy called my name so I wouldn't be late to school. "Daddy, I don't want to go to school. Please don't make me go to school today. I want to be home with Mommy," I said persistently.

"Kesha, your grandma is going to be here when you get home. Get yourself together and get ready and go to school."

I did, but I still felt a burden of sadness in my heart. I knew something was going to happen. I just didn't know what.

As I slowly walked out the door I could hear Grandma's soft voice in my heart, "Kesha, make sure you be careful walking to school."

I cried my eyes out all the way through the park, and at Locust Street I saw Shawn. It seemed as if he came from out of nowhere. I was overwhelmed with fear as he asked me where I was going. He grabbed me by my arm and demanded that I go with him to his sister's house. I knew what he wanted from me. I screamed to get the attention of a man who was sweeping his porch across the street.

"Leave that girl alone before I come over there and put my hands on you," he shouted from his porch.

Those were fighting words to Shawn. "What you say, old man? This is my girl. I can do what I want to her."

The man started walking across the street with his broom in his hands. Shawn let go of my arm, and I ran for my life. I headed toward home with the sound of Shawn and the man arguing fading into the background.

Was Grandma's spirit speaking to me before I left the house that morning, warning me to be careful? No, she was still alive when I left the house. As I reached home I could see my grandfather standing outside smoking his cigarettes, consumed with worry.

"Girl, what are you doing home? I thought I told you to go to school."

"I know, Daddy, but Shawn was messing with me again. He's around the corner fighting with some man."

"Did he put his hands on you?"

"Yes, but I got away and ran home."

"Well, go into the house and help your aunts in the kitchen."

Instead, I ran straight up the steps so I could see my grandma. My Aunt Kim was in the room, and I told her what had happened.

Aunt Kim just shook her head. "Why are you still messing with that boy? Didn't Mommy tell you to leave him alone?"

"He won't let me. He said he will kill me if I leave him alone."

"Kesha, I don't want to discuss this in front of Mommy."

"Mom, I'm here. I came back home to be with you." I spoke softly.

She didn't say a word, just stared at the ceiling.

Aunt Kim drew me from the room and told me that Mommy was not going to get better. "She is dying, and we just have to believe that one day we are all going to see her again in heaven along with your mother and your Aunt Barbara. We are just all here to make her as comfortable as possible."

I ran back into the room, fell to my knees, and cried at her bedside.

"Mommy, why didn't my prayers work? Why won't God heal your body? You said that if I prayed, God would hear me, and answer me. God please don't do this to me. Please help her to get well. I know you could do it. Grandma served you faithfully, so please help her," I pleaded.

God heard my prayers and He answered them according

to His will for my grandmother's life, but I was too young to understand. "I love you, Mommy." I bent down to whisper those words in her ear. "I am sorry for any disrespect I have given you. You are the best thing that ever happened to me. I love you."

Tears poured down my face as she lay there grasping for air. I felt as if I was in a hospital, not my own home. The sounds of machines and the smells of bodily fluids surrounded us. Aunt Kim came into the room, and I ran downstairs, burying my face in the pillows because I didn't want anyone to see me cry so hard.

Moments later Aunt Kim came to the steps and looked at me with an apology in her eyes. "Everyone, please come upstairs; I have to tell you all something," she said.

My aunts and my grandfather gathered around. Mommy was gone. She took her last breath just a moment after I went downstairs. Everyone in the room wept. My heart felt as if it had dropped out of me. I couldn't move; all I could do was stare at her lifeless body in the bed. If only I could hear her voice one more time: I would change the many times I'd made her mad, I would take her advice. My heart was sad, but I could shed no more tears, instead I was filled with anger. Friday, April 30, 1993, at 3:05 p.m., my grandmother took her last breath.

Did Grandma wait to take her last breath until I left the room, knowing I could not have handled seeing her die? I believe she did, but only God knows the answer to my question. That entire day I kept to myself. I couldn't bear to know that I no longer would be able to touch her, hear her call my name, or that I would be able to call on her and she would answer. Grandma was gone, but her words of love, encouragement, wisdom, and understanding would forever live in my heart. I would often hear her voice say, "Baby, my wings were ready. I fought a good fight, now it's time for Grandma to fly."

2 Timothy 4:7: I have fought the good fight, I have finished the race, I have kept the faith.

17. Missing you

I had to be alone to figure out who I really was and what I really wanted out of life. I had no goals, I had no plans for my future. I had no clue to where I wanted to be. All I wanted was to be alone to see where life would take me.

Life without Grandma was different for me, and for my grandfather as well. I had never been as close to my grandfather as I was to Grandma, but we had a growing relationship. I knew that he loved me and cared about what happened to me. Shortly after Grandma's death I began to date Shawn again. The beatings didn't stop; they got worse. I was Shawn's punching bag, someone he walked all over, and I allowed it because I thought I didn't deserve any better.

Shortly after my grandmother's passing, I became sick to the point I couldn't keep any food or liquids down. I could not walk and my abdomen was filled with pain.

"Daddy, I don't feel good. I'm so sick." Part of my body was hot and other parts were cold. *God, what is going on with me?* My temperature was 102 degrees, and I could barely move to get out of bed. Daddy panicked and called my Aunt Kim to tell her what was happening, and she

Never Settle for Less

suggested I go to the nearest emergency room.

"Kesha, are you pregnant?" Daddy asked.

"No, Daddy, why do you ask?"

"Because I had a dream about fish and someone in this family is pregnant." I shook my head. "That does not mean that I am pregnant."

"Well, I hope you're not because you promised your grandma you would finish school and make something of yourself. Besides, there is no room in this house for any babies. Shawn is the wrong person to be having some baby with."

"I know, Daddy, trust me I'm not." Having kids was far from my mind.

Daddy drove me to Helen Fuld Medical Center, and I was quickly rushed to a room where the doctors and nurses on duty examined me. I was so afraid that I was going to die. My body was so cold. *God, I'm not ready to die.* I looked over at Daddy as he sat in the chair with his hands folded and legs crossed. I could tell he was nervous as the nurses took blood and began to hook me up to an IV.

"Mr. Williams, could we talk to you alone for a few minutes?" the doctor asked.

"Is she going to be okay?" Daddy asked nervously.

"Yes, but we need to run more tests to see where the infection is coming from."

All I could do was lie there curled up in a ball in pain. The bright lights in the room helped keep my body warm. The pain was worse than cramps. It felt like a thousand knives were cutting into me. As time went by my aunts slowly began to come to the hospital to check on me and Daddy because he didn't want to leave me alone without knowing what was wrong.

"The doctors say she has an infection somewhere," he

whispered to my aunts.

After many tests and x-rays the doctors decided I required surgery.

My family stood by the entire time, encouraging and praying for me.

The next day I was headed for surgery where I was met by a team of doctors and nurses.

"Don't worry, Kesha, you are going to be just fine. I will be right here when you wake up," Aunt Kim spoke softly.

The only thing I remember about the surgery is lying on the table and a nurse holding my hand and asking me to count backward from ten. I don't remember anything after that.

After hours of surgery I lay in the recovery room. I had a dream I could see myself lying on the hospital bed with my eyes closed. The nurses were at their stations writing notes. My Aunt Barbara, who had died two years after my mother, was surrounded by bright lights as she looked over a balcony at me and smiled. She then tossed a penny into my mouth and before I knew it, I woke up coughing and grabbing my throat. The nurses ran over to help me, saying they had been worried because I had taken so long to wake up.

I stayed in the hospital for several days before being released. I felt Aunt Barbara had been sent to wake me up, and that God had given me another chance at life because of my grandmother's prayers. I had a six-inch scar on my abdomen to remind me of how much mercy God had shown when I was sick. The doctors said if I hadn't gone to the emergency room that night I could have died.

They also said there was a slight chance that I would not be able to have any children because of the surgery. Those words stuck with me for a very long time. I knew that one day I wanted to get married and have children; could this

NEVER SETTLE FOR LESS

be a sign from God that it was time for me to get my life together and leave Shawn alone?

Shortly after the surgery Shawn decided to end our relationship. He told me that he had someone else he was dating and he no longer wanted to keep their relationship a secret. Did he leave peacefully? No, that wasn't his way. He took everything that I had in my room—clothes, jewelry, shoes and more, and placed them in a garbage bag. As he walked out the door he spit in my face and attempted to throw me down the steps. Luckily, my grandfather came in the door just in time, threatening to "put a hot one" in him if he didn't leave.

Shawn was always afraid of my grandfather, so he let me go and ran out the door, leaving everything that he had packed up behind. That day was the end of my horrible, abusive relationship with Shawn and the beginning of a healing process for me. I had to be alone to figure out who I really was and what I really wanted out of life. I had no goals, I had no plans for my future. I had no clue to where I wanted to be. All I wanted was to be alone to see where life would take me. Dating was out of the question because I was fearful of someone wanting to hurt me and take advantage of me. *How could I heal from all this pain?* I wondered. Out of nowhere I heard my grandmother's voice in my heart, "Time, Baby, it's going to take time."

Jeremiah 17:14: Oh Lord, you alone can heal me, you along can save me. My praises are for you alone!.

18. A TIME FOR EVERYTHING

Time taught me how to love myself: the good, the bad, and the growing. It taught me to never settle for less.

How do you know when you're ready to move on with your life? The answer to that question for me was time. Grandma would often say that time heals all wounds. Was it possible for time to heal what was so badly broken and damaged in me: my self-esteem, self-confidence, my love and trust?

Time taught me how to love myself: the good, the bad, and the growing. It taught me to work diligently toward making the necessary changes through self-evaluation, prayer, and the love and support of family and friends. It taught me how to respect myself and carry myself as a young lady deserving of admiration.

I realize we all have something that we wish we could change about ourselves, but learning how to accept those things that were different made me appreciate my life even more.

Did I continue to make mistakes and fall short along the way? Yes, but the wisdom and life lessons I gained along the way helped me to become the woman I am today. I would often ask myself, *were the days of my life previously mapped out by God? Why so much pain? Were my steps ordered by Him? And if so, where would I end?* Only time could answer those questions. "Watch, listen, and learn," were my grandparents' favorite words, I often find myself using them as I journey through life.

After graduating from high school my heart was set on going to college, but the thought of someone making fun of me or laughing at me if I told them that I wanted to go to college to become a teacher crippled me. To make matters worse, I was told by someone close to me that college was not a good fit for someone like me. "College is for smart kids, Kesha, not for people like you. Those kids will make fun of you, and you don't want to be made fun of, do you?" If that person only knew how their words set me back for years, they probably would have just kept their mouth shut.

So instead of going to college, I worked as a movie theater cashier for two years, and then for one year as a dietary aide in a nursing home serving breakfast, lunch, and dinner to patients, as well as often washing dishes. Life was rough, and it was challenging; this was not the life I dreamed of. After jumping from job to job I finally ended up working around the clock at a group home in Ewing, New Jersey, just to make ends meet. Thank God I didn't have any children at the time. It was just me, and I was still living at home with my grandfather. Talk about planning out your future! I knew I was indeed settling for less in every area of my life. I just didn't have the willpower to jump- start my life in the right direction, and I didn't have anyone close to me to point me in the right direction. I would often hear that soft sweet voice in my heart saying, "There is so much more to life, Baby, than this. You have to try, just try harder, Baby." Though

Kesha Cox

Grandma wasn't there physically, she was still speaking to me from above. Was there more to life than this? Did I have what it takes to go to college and become successful? Yes, but lack of courage and fear kept me from achieving my dreams.

※

It was my night off from work, after working doubles all week. I wanted to relax, order a pizza, and lie in the bed. When the phone rang I was hesitant to answer because I knew it was somebody looking for me to drive them somewhere.

"Hey Kesha, what you doing tonight?"

"Nothing. Just relaxing. Why?"

"Because I wanted to know if you want to go to the movies or maybe out to dinner. I have a baby sitter, so come on. You never do anything fun for yourself besides work all the time."

Working around the clock did seem to keep me out of trouble.

"Well, okay, I'll see you in about thirty minutes."

I hung up the phone and yelled down the hallway, "Daddy, don't wait up for me. I'm going to the movies with Terri tonight, so I will see you later."

"Okay, make sure you lock the door behind you."

Daddy was always worried about somebody sneaking into his house, stealing something while he was upstairs. I quickly jumped in the shower, flat ironed my hair, and put on my blush, my favorite nude lipstick, black and grey eye shadow, and mascara. Rushing through my closet looking for something to wear, I grabbed a pair of fitted blue jeans and my red, ruffled hem top. Quickly rushing downstairs and out the door, I noticed a tall, dark-skinned guy standing next door talking with my neighbor. He was about six-feet two-inches tall and built like he was training for football; his body was lean, and every muscle made a statement as it gleaned through his white ribbed t-shirt.

Oh my god, who is this guy? I've never seen him around here before.

"Hey Kesha, what's up?" my neighbor shouted.

"I'm running late for my movie, "I said, laughing, and out of nowhere I heard, "Can I go with you?"

Um yes you can! But my more cautious self just laughed and replied, "Maybe next time."

"Okay, I'm gonna hold you to your word."

Rushing to get Terri, so I wouldn't hear her complain about being late, I couldn't get the image of that fine tall body out of my head. *Lawd, please let him still be there talking when I get back home tonight.*

"About time you got here. Hurry up and pull off before my mom comes out here complaining about babysitting. What took you so long?" Terri asked.

"Girl, please, I was distracted by something that only heaven could have created."

"What's his name?"

"I don't know yet, but I will find out when I get back home."

Tired from the night before, I woke up early in the morning with the image of that fine, dark-skinned guy I had seen the day before. All I thought about from the moment I laid eyes on him was that I hoped he was single, and I was not wasting my time on something that would cause me problems.

I heard dogs barking and voices outside talking and laughing. I thought it could be him, so I ran downstairs and looked out the window. It was my grandfather and his friends, Mr. Bart, and Mr. Vincent, the three men who saw everything that went on in Faircrest. They were the Neighborhood Watch Crew. Nothing was able to get past them. If you did something wrong, within hours your parents were going to find out, and it was over from there.

"Good morning, Mr. Bart, good morning. Hey Mr. Vincent."

"Hey Kee, how you doing this morning?"

"I'm good, about to get ready for work."

Daddy slowly turned around in his chair. "Kesha, today is rent day, remember?"

"Yes, Daddy, I remember. I'll have your rent tomorrow when I cash my check."

"Okay, just making sure," Daddy replied.

Daddy didn't play when it came to owing him money. He wanted every penny or he would charge interest. At the same time, he was so funny I couldn't help but laugh when he asked for his money. Cigarettes and money were his two favorite things, and I didn't mind helping with his bills since he was on a fixed income.

It had been almost a year since Mommy had died, and Daddy's and my conversations often ended in arguments. I wanted to live how I wanted to live and not abide by his rules, and he wasn't having it. He would say, "Kesha, you are grown and you can get out of my house if you won't respect my rules." He was right, but my whole life was in that house from the day my mother brought me home from the hospital, and it was hard for me to leave.

Daddy started casually dating other women, and I didn't like it at all. Mommy was the only woman I ever knew in my grandfather's life, and I wasn't having anybody come into our family and try to destroy what my grandma worked so hard to build. Ms. Eva was a short, high yellow lady with a permanent grin on her face who expressed how she felt about anybody who came across her path. She didn't bite her tongue or hold back words about how she felt about a person, and neither did I. I didn't hold back how I felt about her. We were at war every time she stepped foot into our house. I was on a mission to get rid of her.

I didn't like Ms. Eva for my grandfather because I felt she was too bossy, and I wasn't having nobody take advantage of him. So I did everything in my power to separate them, and Daddy disliked that. Our relationship with each other was a raging war at that point. He threatened to put me out if I didn't stop interfering with his relationship with Ms. Eva.

"I was faithful to your grandmother and took good care of her up until she died, so let me be! I have a right to live my life. You need to get a life of your own," he yelled.

"Daddy, you're right, but Ms. Eva is something else. I don't like her! Yes, you are old enough to make decisions about your relationships, but Ms. Eva just rubs me the wrong way. It's something about her that just makes the hairs on the back of my neck stand up."

"Here you are sounding just like your grandmother, always perceiving things about people. Ms. Eva is fine, just let me live my life. I'm going to be okay. That's why I have your aunts around to make sure Ms. Eva is treating me right and with respect. They won't let her get away with anything," Daddy said sternly.

Why couldn't he just understand that it was hard for me to accept what he was doing? "Kesha, just let it go and let your grandfather live his life; he will be fine." I heard my grandmother's voice as clearly as if she was standing right in front of me.

The next day I was so sorry and ashamed about what had happened that I walked downstairs to the kitchen table, where Daddy sat drinking his coffee and reading the newspaper, and apologized to him.

"Kesha, I been on this earth much longer than you. I know when someone is trying to hurt me and play me as a fool. I'm not some crazy old man, you know. Don't you worry about me, just worry about yourself."

"Okay," I said, shaking my head as I walked away from the kitchen table.

༄

Weeks went by and still no sign of the hot guy I'd seen at my neighbor's house. I guessed it wasn't meant for me to see him again. But dang, he was fine.

Every so often I would go out on dates, trying to find someone suitable. I was tired of being alone and watching my girlfriends enjoy their relationships with their boyfriends. The healing process was over after my relationship with Shawn; I was ready to move on.

Some dates were set up by my friends and others were men I met myself. Freddy was my first date and the most concerning relationship ever. He was a straight-up momma's boy; everything that we did included his mother. He could never make up his mind without consulting his mother. If we went out to eat he had to check with his mother. If he came to my house he had to check with his mother. He was twenty-one and I was eighteen, but he was still tied to his momma's apron strings. He would invite me to dinner at his house when his mother cooked, and every time she would lecture me at the dinner table on not getting pregnant because her son wasn't ready for children.

After Freddy I found myself dating men just for the sake of dating. I worked, had my own money, and supported myself; I was fine living the single life. If I ever came across Mr. Right he had to be everything that I wanted him to be. I wanted a man who was smart, charming, well mannered, one who treated me with respect and loved me for who I was. And having a job was a must. I was not going to waste any time on a relationship that wasn't going anywhere and wouldn't benefit me in the long run.

There were times I would sit back and think about how Shawn treated me, and my heart would slowly harden, because I felt he took my kindness as a weakness, my love as something to play with, my emotions as a playground, and I had had enough. I was becoming bitter and angry all over again. Grandma always said hurt people always hurt other people, and she was right. I felt as if I wanted to hurt every man who came across my path.

After months of dating, in and out of relationships, I was growing tired of the dating game. I just wanted to call it quits. Then out of nowhere, while sitting on my porch fixing my shoe, he walked by and said hi. *Oh my god it's him!* His body has even more muscles than before. Should I ask him his name?

"Hi," I shouted back, "What's your name?"

He stopped and smiled and told me his name was Byron and said maybe we could go out sometime.

"My birthday is coming up in a few weeks, maybe we could go then," I replied.

Weeks went by and Byron was back knocking at my door asking me out for my birthday. I had some doubts at first because he looked like he had a lot of game with him. I couldn't for the life of me figure out why this man was single because he was so fine. He had everything that a woman like me could ask for. He was smooth, charming, and smart; whatever he put his mind to do he would carry out. People say diamonds are a girl's best friend, and Byron shone bright, just like one.

Kesha Cox

Was I moving too fast? I was so afraid of what might happen if I gave him my heart. I had to put my past relationships behind me so that I could grow in this relationship. *Okay, Byron, I'm about to give you my heart, but please don't break it.* This relationship changed my life for the better. Byron helped me appreciate the life I have today. He was someone everyone knew and loved. He was a nice person, but I knew he had game, and I knew what I was getting myself into. Byron was known for living the fast life, and I was still quiet, shy, and laid back. I fell so quickly in love with him. Nobody could tell me anything bad about this man. He was my life, my heart; he was my Byron.

What did I learn from my relationship with Shawn? Did I learn how not to settle for less in any relationship? Did I learn how to love myself and appreciate who I was as a person? I didn't learn it well enough, because I soon found myself back in a similar situation; but this time the abuse was mental, which was worse. Byron was seven years older than me, so he seemed a lot more mature when it came to being in relationships. He often made me feel my opinions in the relationship didn't matter and he knew what was best because he was older. When I disagreed with him, he would immediately say I was young-minded and childish and didn't know anything about being an adult. So instead of voicing my opinions or concerns, I would keep silent about how I felt. But he also taught me a lot of great things I needed to know about the streets. I was naive in some things because my grandparents had sheltered me. I didn't have a clue to what was going on around me most of the time, and he had to save me in a number of situations.

If I saw people conducting illegal activities near my street, I would curse them out and tell them to get away from around my house. Byron told me I had to be careful and

Never Settle for Less

mindful of what I said to people because they would hurt me if I interfered with their business. Byron also taught me how to carry myself as a lady and how I should act. He didn't like that disrespectful attitude that sometimes came out in me when I would curse someone out, talk loud, and wear revealing clothing. He was very particular in how he wanted me to act, look, and dress. My heart was opened wide, like a ship that went in and out of its port. Byron was beginning to be my everything.

The fast life that he lived was of little concern to me, because he was careful in what he did and how he did it. "No worries, Kesha, I got this," he would say as he went to handle his business. There were some nights I felt safe, but some nights I didn't know if I was ever going to see him again. "Kesha, what are you doing? I raised you better than this," I would hear in my heart. But this time I ignored the voice because I wanted to be with Byron. He made me feel needed and sometimes special.

Byron told me he had a son, but had ended his relationship with the boy's mother. I thought I wasn't messing around with just any man, but someone who actually knew about the importance of family. Could this relationship get any better? Some of the men I knew had children and didn't care for any of them, but Byron was different. He took good care of his son. And I spent as much time with the child as Byron allowed. We were becoming a little family, and that meant the world to me. I didn't want to lose it.

Byron was very conscious about how he did things, he didn't like a lot of people knowing his business, but I was different. My family and I had a close relationship, and I told certain aunts everything. Byron didn't like that. I was twenty when we met, and he was twenty-seven.

"Kesha, the lifestyle that I live is way too fast for you, and there are some things you will never understand."

My heart was saddened, but I knew he was right. His lifestyle was way too much for me to handle, but there was a part of me that was willing to take a risk to be with him, so I compromised my morals and values, everything I believed in, and convinced Byron to stay with me. I worked on changing into what he wanted me to be. Because I wanted to make him happy. I would do things for him I knew weren't right and could cost me my freedom. I knew what I was getting myself into, and still I played the part he wanted me to play. Not once did I consider my feelings in the relationship because my only desire was to please him.

Shortly after settling down with Byron I became pregnant. I was happy and excited. I felt God had shown me mercy because the doctors hadn't been sure I would be able to have children after my surgery. But there was a part of me that was afraid to tell my family, let alone tell Byron. He had made it clear that he didn't want any more kids at the time because he was dealing with so much in his life.

When I told him I was pregnant, his first response to me was "I told you I wasn't ready for any more kids." I told him I would not do away with having my baby and if I had to take care of it all by myself I would. Was having this baby going to keep Byron in my life? Would he leave me because I was having his child? Would it help change his mind and outlook on life? Only time would tell.

Knowing that I was pregnant made me ready to make some changes in my lifestyle. My life was no longer about me, but about the little one who was growing inside me. I made my family aware of my pregnancy and my relationship with Byron. I was old enough to make my own decisions, so my family didn't bother me much. I was still living with my grandfather, and he was not pleased with my choice of settling for less in my relationship with Byron. "Kesha, your grandmother and I raised you well, why do you keep settling for these no-good men? You should want better out of life. You are at the age where you could care for yourself. If Byron loves you he will take the responsibility to care for you and find y'all a place to live." Daddy was right. It was time for me to move out and experience life on my own.

I told Byron that I was going to have to move out of my grandfather's house and he was going to have to care for me and his child, and he did just that. He found us a place to live so we could raise our son; he was indeed a family man, but his priorities regarding life were still in the wrong place. While I was pregnant, Byron got into some major trouble with the law and had to serve some jail time. The judge agreed that he would sentence Byron after the baby was born, and I was thankful for that, because I was afraid of raising our son on my own. I didn't want to be a single mother. I had seen what other single mothers were going through. I wanted my son to have his father in his life, so I settled for whatever I had to do in order to keep my family together. I accepted the good and the bad about Byron. There were plenty of nights I spent crying in my bed because I didn't know if he was ever going to come home. I worried someone would maybe shoot him, rob him, or that he would be caught by the police and locked up.

What was I to do? Should I leave, or should I stay in this relationship? I always answered yes, even when I knew that the relationship wasn't healthy. Many women choose to stay in relationships that will end up leading to a dead end because they lack self-confidence, or feel they are not worthy of being loved or deserving of more. I didn't realize until years later that my life was worth so much more than having a fine piece next to me.

Life lessons are sometimes hard to learn when your vision is cloudy and your heart is not yet healed from past hurts and broken relationships. The constant drama with other women, the drugs, the cheating, the constant fast pace of the street life, and the continuous company of friends who were bad influences to both our personal lives and relationship are what I accepted to be a normal everyday life.

My grandma always said everything in your life is a reflection of a choice you have made. If you want a different result, make a different choice.

Proverbs 11:14: Without wise leadership, a nation falls; with many counselors there is safety.

19. A MOTHER'S LOVE

Having a baby was a life-changer for me. It gave me a whole new perspective on life. Kawan, you are heaven sent. The one who God sent to light up the stars in my sky. You are a life-changer, a lifesaver, and I love you.

No words could express how I felt the day I was told that I was pregnant. My heart leaped with excitement when the doctor said, "You are going to be a mommy."

I was going to give life to another. Things were going to have to change for the better because of the life I was bringing into this world. After attending several doctor appointments an ultrasound revealed certain health risks I could encounter while giving natural birth. "Ms. Williams, after looking over the ultrasound and conducting tests, we recommended that you have a C-section, because we are afraid of placing you and the baby at risk during the delivery." My heart began to pound rapidly as if it was going to explode.

The doctor recommended bed rest, which meant giving up my full-time job and staying at home during the remainder of my pregnancy. Byron would have to carry the full load of the bills, which meant he would never be home, and that thought had me worried sick.

The first time I felt my baby move inside me I was lying across the bed watching the Jerry Springer show. It was the weirdest thing I have ever felt. I got up and ran into the living room with excitement to tell Byron.

He jumped off the couch and placed his hand on my belly; I felt a slight kick. He smiled, placed both hands on me, and the baby moved again.

Kawan would move back and forth across my belly as if he was swimming a marathon. We both were so amazed that something so small could move so fast. "Kawan" was the name his father named him, and it fit him so well. Kawan had a mind of his own even before he was born. He would curl into a tight knot on the right side of my belly, as if he was hiding from someone. I would tap my belly several times for him to move to the other side so that I could lay down and rest. I knew he would be a very active child.

Finally, my baby boy was on his way! I was scheduled for my C-section on Tuesday, December 9. We were both so excited we couldn't even sleep the night before and were up bright and early.

"Kesha, it's time to get up so you can deliver my son," he said, and I laughed because he sounded just like a kid in a candy store. "If Kawan is anything like his father, I have my work cut out for me," I laughed to myself.

We arrived at the hospital 6:30 in the morning, and I was suddenly consumed with fear. I didn't know what to expect. What if something happened to the baby? What if something went wrong? Thank God the doctors were helpful and encouraging.

In my room a nurse hooked me up to a machine to monitor Kawan's heartbeat. "Are you ready to meet this little ray of sunshine who's been so excitedly moving around this morning?" she asked.

"Yes, I am," I shouted.

As I was escorted to the delivery room my doctor was there in surgical mask and blue scrubs. When she asked me if I was ready to be a mommy, I hesitated to answer. It all hit me at once. My mother was not here. My grandmother was not here. Would I be a good mother? Who would I go to for advice? "Lord, I need your help," I prayed. And out of nowhere a sense of peace came over me. "Shh, child, I'm right here with you, you will be just fine," I heard. It had to be Grandma speaking to my heart.

It gave me the strength of a lion. "Yes, Dr. Smith, I'm ready to meet my baby boy," I said.

As the anesthesiologist slid a needle into my lower back to administer the epidural, everything in my lower body went numb. I could feel the pressure as the doctors pulled, and soon Kawan had arrived, crying at the top of his lungs. He weighed five pounds, eleven ounces, and was born at 9:20 a.m.

Byron was the first person to hold him. He hugged him and touched him, and it was easy to see that he was happy and felt protective about his tiny son. Kawan was safe in his father's arms. Tears fell from my eyes. Giving birth to a healthy baby boy was the best gift I had ever experienced.

Byron, wearing his blue scrubs, handed me Kawan. "Kesha, look at our little man man. He looks just like his big brother," he said, referring to Byron's oldest child.

Kawan was a light-skinned version of his older brother and his father. His little ears were peeling, and his skin was as soft as cotton. He looked so innocent and pure as he stared into my eyes. He looked like he didn't have a care in the world.

Kesha Cox

Having a baby was a life-changer for me. It gave me a whole new perspective on life. From that moment I promised God I would do right by my boy and make better choices in life. Nothing in the world would be able to break this bond between my son and myself. He was my angel sent from God, and it was my responsibility to care for him and protect him, just like my grandparents protected and cared for me.

My family was excited to welcome the new addition. When he would smile I could hear my grandmother say that the angels were laughing and talking with him. "And Kesha, he is enjoying their every word."

Of course, once Kawan was born it was time for Byron to serve his jail time. It was a sad and depressing moment. I knew he was going to miss out on a lot of the early stages of Kawan's life; things that were important to me such as his first words, the first time he crawled and walked, his first birthday party. Byron was going to miss it all.

I made sure we went to visit him in jail and wrote letters and sent pictures as often as I could. Was this the life I wanted, going back and forth to prison visiting Byron with our son? But he promised this would be the last time he would ever go to jail; he wanted to be a father to his children, and having a family meant everything to him. Did I believe him? A part of me wanted too.

Jeremiah 1:5: I knew you before I formed you in your mother's womb. Before you were born I set you apart and appointed you as my spokesman to the world.

20. Lord, help Me, I'm Drowning

*God, please help me with this child,
I don't want to live my life this way.*

Times were hard for me when Byron left to serve his time in jail. I had no income coming in; I was surviving off my savings, and that account was almost empty. I had to think of something quick because the bills were piling up, the rent was behind, shut-off notices were coming in the mail from the cable company, phone company, and electric company. I didn't have enough money to pay my car insurance so I had to be careful how and where I drove my car. Everything was falling apart.

Kawan was only eight weeks old when I had to return to work. My hours were hectic and long; I would work from 2 to 10 p.m. every Monday through Wednesday and every weekend. Officially, I had Thursdays and Fridays off, but if someone called out of work I would go in just to get the extra money to keep food on the table and to get Kawan the things he needed.

Kesha Cox

Working all hours of the day and night made me feel like a terrible mother. I was hardly home to raise him. When I would get off at 10:00 p.m. I would arrive at my grandfather's house at 10:45 p.m., wrap Kawan up in his blankets, and head home. Some nights it would be bitter cold outside, with snow and ice everywhere. Kawan stayed sick with colds, high fevers, and ear infections. Often having to take him to the emergency room sickened me. But I had to make a living for my son. Living from paycheck to paycheck I never had enough money. My paychecks were often short because I would have to call off work because Kawan was sick. I often had to ask my grandfather for money. *God, please help me with this child, I don't want to live my life this way.*

Thank God for my grandfather, Aunt Carolyn, cousins, and the rest of my family, who took good care of my baby while I worked all hours of the day and night just to make ends meet. My family helped teach Kawan many things. From potty training to walking, you name it, they did it.

I received my eviction notice one week from the end of the month. I had to be out of my apartment by then or the rental office would padlock the doors.

"What am I going to do?" I wondered. Would Daddy turn me away because I'd left on bad terms with him over his dating Ms. Eva?

The next day I called my stepmother (my father had married in 1985) and told her what has happening. She got a team of men together to help me move out of the apartment. I placed our belongings in storage and went to see my grandfather. All morning long I rehearsed what I would say to him.

"Daddy, I'm in a tight place right now, so I need to move back home for a little while, at least until I can get back on my feet. Please don't turn me away," I asked nervously.

Did he mind having us back home? No, but he made sure he laid down the house rules before letting us move back in.

"Now, Kesha I'm going to let you come back home, but you will not tell me what to do in my own house. You will pay rent and whatever else I ask you to pay."

Daddy was tough on the outside, but he had a soft heart. I knew he loved us and wanted the best for us, but he didn't play any games. I had to pay my portion of the rent, clean the house every weekend, and buy my own food.

After months of living back home with Daddy I was ready to go. Everywhere I turned a cloud of cigarette smoke hit me in my face, and my clothes reeked of Winston 100s. I didn't want Kawan around any cigarette smoke because it could lead to more health problems.

"Daddy, can you please do me a favor and smoke outside?" I asked him one day while preparing to go to work.

"Oh hell, this smoke isn't gone hurt you or Kawan. If you don't like my smoking, then get out!"

He would sit at the dinner table with his black-chipped coffee mug, news channel blasting, legs crossed, wearing his favorite green cargo pants and grey sweatshirt with tiny burn holes from his cigarettes. Puffing his poisonous smoke into the air, he would hum as he took each puff. The white walls leading to the second floor of the house had to be repainted every summer because they were so yellow from the nicotine.

Daddy was a piece of work when it came to his cigarettes, money, and coffee, so to avoid any arguments I would shake my head, kiss my son, and walk out of the door for work. Yes, he was stubborn, but his house was always a place of shelter for loved ones who needed a place to stay or

KESHA COX
call home. He never turned anyone away.

Psalm 91: 1-2: Those who live in the shelter of the Most High will find rest in the shadows of the Almighty. This I will declare of the Lord, "He is my refuge, my place of safety, He is my God, and I am trusting him.

21. WAS IT WORTH WAITING?

God, I don't understand, but I know you make no mistakes.

The year passed. Byron was released from jail, and we were ready to start our lives over again. I thought that things would be better for us once he got himself together. I thought being away from us would do him good. I was wrong; a week after he got out of jail, Byron was back at it again, hustling in the streets.

I wanted my son to have his father in his life, but I was not willing to stay and deal with the drama that followed him: coming in and out of the house at all hours, bad company, friends over every night, dealing with the emotional abuse again, Byron talking to me any kind of way, my kindness being taken for granted. And worst of all, I didn't know for sure if he was keeping drugs in the house, even though I had asked him not to for the welfare and safety of our son.

Yes, I'd had enough, but I still didn't have the courage to leave. I loved this man, but we were two different people going in two different directions. I wanted to settle down and be a real family where both parents worked and where each person wanted what was best for the other. But that can only happen if both people want the same thing. My grandmother had said "to love is to let go." I wasn't ready to let go.

After a few months back at home Byron decided we should purchase a home together in the Chambersburg area of Trenton. He had always wanted his own home, so he decided that if we were going to try and be a family, we should start by getting a place of our own. It was an attached row house with two bedrooms, kitchen, dining room, living room, and a wooden deck. It was a dream come true for the both of us, especially with raising Kawan and Byron's older son. The area was family-oriented, quiet, and friendly.

On the day of the real estate closing I felt so good to own a home at the age of twenty-one; the youngest in my family to ever be a homeowner. The mortgage was in my name, of course, but Byron made it clear that he was the man of the house and things would be run the way he wanted.

I had no problem allowing him to be the man of the house, but if he ever fell short I knew how to carry the load and put things back together. I had watched my grandparents over the years and had seen how they worked together to make the best out of what they had.

"Kesha, always have your priorities in order, know what you want out of life, and never depend so much on a man you don't know what to do," my grandmother would say. So when things fell apart I found a way to put them back together. I would work, save, and pay the bills as needed. Having a roof over my family's head was my first priority.

Two months after moving into our new house I found out I was pregnant again. I cried so hard in the doctor's office when she gave me my test results that she asked me what was wrong. And there it was, I broke my silence.

"Dr. Smith, I'm not sure if I want this baby because we

are going through so much in our relationship. I am actually looking for a way out."

"The choice is yours," the doctor told me. "You're eight weeks pregnant, go home, talk about it with your boyfriend and let me know what you decide to do. We have a long history together, so whatever you decide to do I'm in your corner."

I waited for hours until he finally walked through that door, repeating in my mind what and how I was going to tell him that I was pregnant with our second child. I was upstairs watching television, Kawan asleep next to me, when I heard keys jingling in the door and heavy footsteps walking across the living room floor.

"Kesha, where are you? Come downstairs. Did the doctor say you are pregnant?"

When I told him yes he was excited.

"I knew you were; my heart never steers me wrong. Did you tell your family?"

"No, I didn't, and I'm not going to tell anyone because I'm not sure if I want to keep this baby."

"Why would you say that?" he asked angrily. "What do you mean you're not sure if you're going to have my baby? Are you crazy?"

"Byron, I'm not bringing another child into this world knowing that our relationship is on the rocks. I'm not happy living the way you're living. We are barely making ends meet financially, and I'm tired of making excuses why I should stay in this relationship. I never know when you're going to get locked up; I never know when the police are going to come through those doors. I'm tired of the nonsense."

Byron stood about six-feet, two-inches tall, and when he became angry he would wave his hands in every direction and curse up a storm. "Kesha, do whatever you want, but my son will not be going anywhere, so if you want to leave then go, but my kids are staying."

I knew that meant the baby I was carrying, too. My heart was heavy, and my eyes were puffy from crying. *God, what am I going to do about this situation? I can't afford to take care of another baby, and I'm not happy.* Again, out of nowhere, I heard my grandma say, "You made this bed, so you lay in it." I knew what she meant. I'd settled for less, so now I had to deal with it.

That same night I had a dream about my grandmother. I was running up the stairs and I heard my grandmother calling me from her bedroom, "Kesha, Kesha, come into the bedroom." I ran with excitement because I was so happy to see her again. When I entered her bedroom I hugged her, crying, "Mommy, I miss you so much." But she pulled back and began to yell at me, "Get out of here. I'm disappointed in you. I didn't raise you this way. What are you becoming? Get yourself together, young lady, or your life is going to end sooner than what you think."

I woke up in sweat, clinging tightly to the covers of my bed. When I told Byron about the dream, he said, "Why would she be disappointed in you?"

I didn't answer him. I lay in silence because I knew why she was disappointed. I was disappointed in myself, too, for settling for the life I was living. "Grandma," I told her silently, "if you can hear me, I just want to say I am sorry and I pray that you would forgive me for being such a disappointment to you. This baby is growing fast in me and I don't know what to do."

Working around the clock till the midnight hours, my body was tired; every chance I got to rest I would take. One Saturday morning the phone rang. It was the supervisor on-

Never Settle for Less

call requesting that I work from 9 to 4 p.m., because someone called out. I could sure use the overtime.

As I got ready for work, I became light-headed and crampy, as if I were having a period. I called down the hallway to Byron to help me back into the bedroom.

After an hour passed I felt a little better, but the cramps were still there.

"Kesha. are you sure you want to go to work?"

"Yes, I'm sure. I will be okay."

I arrived at work and became so dizzy again that I had to call for assistance. The cramps were coming back to back, and stronger, and I began to spot. This was not normal during pregnancy.

The woman who I worked with, and who knew I was pregnant, helped me to finish the chores I had been assigned at the group home, but I only felt more and more ill.

Then it happened. I had the urge to urinate, and when I went there was blood everywhere. I went to the hospital where the doctors ran tests, took blood samples, and informed me that I was having a miscarriage. I cried as the doctor gave me the news, but my heart felt at peace. *God, I don't understand but I know you make no mistakes.*

As I closed my eyes I saw my grandmother smiling as she said, "It's for a reason, Baby, just trust God."

I called some of my family and asked them to help Byron with Kawan. Soon, Byron arrived. As I heard the nurse outside directing him to my room, I groaned. *God, give me the strength I need to look this man in his face and tell him I'm having a miscarriage.*

"Kesha, what's up? Are you all right? What's wrong with you?"

"The doctor says I'm having a miscarriage."

Byron pulled up a chair and sat down close to me, folded

his hands, put his head down slowly to his lap, and began to cry. I could see the tears falling from his eyes onto the beige floor tiles.

"Byron, baby, I'm sorry," I said as he lifted up his head, sad and hurt. I had never seen him that way before. Did he really care about just what happened to me? Or was it just a show he was putting on? I knew he had feelings, but were they real? He always played the tough guy. But deep inside my heart I knew we weren't ready for another baby.

Proverbs 3:5-6: Trust in the Lord with all your heart; do not depend on your own understanding. Seek his will in all you do, and he will direct your paths.

22. Something strange is happening

*Always trust your instincts;
they will never steer you wrong.*

Weeks passed after the miscarriage; my doctor placed me on bed rest so I could heal and recover. I stayed at home, spending countless hours caring for Kawan. Things were peaceful, yet strange. I began to notice that every time I answered the house phone the person on the other end would hang up. I would say, "Hello, hello," and would hear someone breathing on the other end of the line. But there was never a reply. What is going on? Who was playing on my phone?

The next time it rang Byron was on the other end.

"Did you just call here and hang up?"

"No, why?"

I explained that someone has been calling every few hours, breathing hard into the receiver, but never saying a word.

Byron had no explanation, and we didn't have Caller ID,

so I just let it go, but I wondered if this man was cheating on me. Had he given another woman the house number so she could call him? I was young, but I wasn't anybody's fool. For two weeks straight there were more hang-ups than normal. Sometimes I wouldn't answer the phone. One day while sweeping the leaves off the porch I noticed a white Ford Focus parked across the street. A woman sat in the driver's seat, her window slightly down, with a camera, taking pictures in the direction of our home.

"Hey," I yelled, "What are you doing taking pictures of our house? What are you doing around here?"

She started her engine and pulled beside me.

"My name is Heather, and I work for a local real estate broker. I was just taking pictures of the homes on this block. They are so beautiful and well-kept. How long have you lived on this street?"

"What? I'm sorry. Who are you again?" She repeated the same information.

"Oh yes, we have very nice homes here, and the neighbors are very friendly," I replied.

But something told me this woman was not who she said she was. Was she trying to buy drugs? Maybe I should keep talking to her to find out just what she wanted.

"Excuse me, Heather, are you going to be selling any homes around here anytime soon?" I asked.

"Yes, there's a house on the next block that will be going up for sale soon."

As she was talking I made sure I got a good look at her, just in case anything happened. She was small in build, about five feet, four inches in height and dressed very well in a purple wrap dress and thin high heels.

Kawan began to cry in the background.

"Oh, you have a baby?"

"Yes, I do. Well, he's not a baby anymore. He's growing like a weed."

She laughed lightly. "Well, I'll let you get to your mommy duties. It was nice talking with you."

As I slowly closed the door, I noticed her hurrying to her car. She instantly picked up her cell phone and called someone, pointing to the house.

Something strange was happening. This woman was no real estate broker. Why hadn't I asked for some ID?

Byron returned home later that night, and I told him what had happened.

"She's probably just some newbie trying to work her way up in the real estate business. Nothing to worry about."

And out of nowhere the question blurted out of my mouth. "Byron, do you have drugs in this house?"

"What are you talking about?"

"Do you have any drugs in this house?"

"Kesha, no, I promised you I wouldn't bring anything like that around my family."

"I hope you are telling me the truth."

Where had that question come from? It just flowed from out my mouth as if I didn't have any control over what I was saying. And Byron, the entire night, seemed to be uneasy and nervous.

"Baby, what's wrong?" I asked.

"Nothing. It's rough out there in the street. There's no money coming in. Man, I need to get a job, and fast, so I can take care of my family."

Colossians 4:2: Devote yourselves to prayer with an alert mind and a thankful heart.

23. When it all ended

If you aren't being treated with love and respect, check your price tag. Maybe you've marked yourself down. It's YOU who tells people what your worth is. Get off of the clearance rack and get behind the glass where they keep the valuables.

I heard a loud noise outside my window. Voices saying, "Open up the door! This is the police!"

Okay, Kesha, you're dreaming, go back to sleep. But those voices became even clearer, and I knew they were at my front door. There were police cars everywhere, and all I could say to Byron was "What did you do? Why are you doing this?"

I opened the door for the police; there were guns pointed directly at my face, telling me to get on the ground.

"Where is he?" they shouted.

"He's upstairs. Please, don't hurt my baby," I pleaded. My son, only nineteen months old, stood at the top of the steps, in tears, with his hands reaching for me.

At that moment I promised I would not let anyone hurt him ever again. I knew I would neither risk my life, nor my son's life, for this foolishness. My grandparents hadn't done this to me, and I wasn't going to put my son through any more pain, not even the pain of his own father.

I felt shame and guilt as the police rushed through my home with guns drawn and their dogs barking. It was late October; the doors were all open, and the house was so cold that one of the police officers gave me a blanket to put over Kawan. My neighbors stood looking on in amazement as Byron was escorted to the car in handcuffs. *What am I going to do? What am I going to say about what took place here today?* Looks of disapproval were plain on the faces of the police officers as they walked back and forth throughout the house.

"Ms. Williams, please have a seat. We need to ask you a few questions," one of the officers said.

"Okay," I replied nervously.

"We have been watching Byron for a while now. We have evidence that can put him away for a very long time."

The detectives began to show me pictures of the house, me outside sweeping the leaves off the porch, talking to my neighbors, Kawan playing with me on the porch.

"Wait," I thought, *"these pictures look familiar."* Then I remembered the realtor taking pictures of the house a few days before. I had known something wasn't right with her.

"Are there any drugs in the house?"

"No, no, there's not," I replied angrily.

"Are you sure, because we are going to search this house from top to bottom and if we find any drugs you are going to jail. Is there anyone we can call to take your son?"

"Yes, my grandfather, but why? There are no drugs in this house."

Was I certain there were no drugs in the house? No, but Byron had promised me he wouldn't bring any of that mess around our family. God, I hoped he was true to his word.

After an hour-long search of everything I considered personal to me, the police came up empty-handed. There were no drugs inside the house or in my car. Once everyone cleared out of my home I sat with Kawan in a dark corner in my living room and cried. No mother would ever want her child to experience what my son and I had just gone through. Kawan wouldn't stop crying because he was afraid. I made a decision right there to make a better life for him. If I didn't the next time the police came to the door, they might just be taking me out in a body bag.

The very next day the incident hit the front page of both *The Trenton Times* and *The Trentonian*. Byron was not the only drug dealer in the city arrested that day. A lot of dealers were rounded up and brought in, and the streets were quiet for a few weeks because no one trusted anyone with their business.

After months of going back and forth to court and long-drawn-out attorney pleas, Byron was sentenced to ten years of federal prison time on drug charges. I would visit Byron in jail, taking my baby with me; but it wasn't the same. I wanted more out of life than this. I wanted out, but couldn't find the way to say it. *The time will present itself soon Kesha if you would just listen and take heed.* The voice in my heart spoke. God knows that I was tired of the fast life. I loved Byron so much, but I had a choice to make, and I knew that choice had to be to let him go. It was hard, but it was the best thing for me.

I could hear Grandma saying those words again, "Kesha, to love is to let go." The hurt and the pain were unbearable at times, so I put that energy into caring for my son and working. I focused on one thing, and one thing only: my baby boy. I wanted the best for him and for me, so I did what I had to do in order to create the lifestyle I wanted for both of us.

※

I remember that morning so clearly because the mirror attached to my bedroom dresser fell and cracked into pieces. I had just picked Kawan up from off the bed and walked into the bathroom, and we both heard a loud noise and glass shattering. Just then, the phone rang. It was Byron.

"I miss my family," he told me. "I wish I was home, but hopefully with good behavior I will be released very soon."

I had heard those words before.

"Okay, that sounds great," I said in a less than enthusiastic voice, all the time saying to myself, "Now is the time, Kesha. Tell him how you really feel."

"Byron, we need to talk about our relationship. I'm not happy, and I want to move on with my life. I can't do this anymore. I love you, but I can't continue to live this life, not for me and not for Kawan."

"Are you seeing someone else?" he asked. "Do you have my son around another man?"

I paused, I was nervous about how to answer. I could tell Byron wasn't happy, and I knew his heart was broken. But what about my heart? I was tired of disregarding how I really felt to please and make somebody else happy. It was my time for me to be happy and enjoy life.

Was I dating someone at the time? No. But I knew what I had to say in order for him to let go.

"Promise me one thing, Kesha. Don't take my son away from me."

"Byron, I promise I won't take Kawan away from you. I will make sure he stays in contact with you."

I didn't hear from Byron for quite a long time after that. Were there nights I would sit and wait for the phone to ring?

KESHA COX

Yes, but my heart kept saying it was time to move on; Byron would be fine. Did I keep my promise to let Kawan stay in contact with his father? No, I did not. I was afraid to visit him because I knew I would go back to him if I did, even if he was behind bars for ten years.

I loved Byron, but enough was enough. My trust in him was broken. My way of showing Byron how much I loved him was to let go and leave. I loved my life too much to stay in a relationship that wasn't going anywhere. I wanted out, and I took the exit door. Would I regret someday Kawan not having a relationship with his father? At the time I was sure that I would, but at that moment it was the only choice I could make. I had to leave in order to find a better life for me and for my son.

Isaiah 40:31: But those who wait on the Lord will find new strength. They will fly high on wings like eagles. They will run and not grow weary. They will walk and not faint.

24. Life or death

Never again would I put myself in a situation where I risked my life just because I desperately wanted to be loved and accepted by a man.

As I continued to work and save my money things slowly came together. I was able to furnish my home, pay my bills, and provide for my son.

Occasionally dating, I was determined not to let down my guard, but then it happened again. I met a man who seemed so sweet. We began dating, but over a few months, as things got deeper between us, I realized that our relationship was based on lies. There was no truth in his mouth. I had had enough!

Why did I keep allowing men to hurt me? Because I didn't know my true worth, I didn't know who I was, and that left a deep dark scar on my heart, allowing me to always settle for less in relationships. At night before going to bed I would pray and ask God to help me find my way, help me find myself. Lo and behold, God did indeed answer my prayer. But not the way I thought he would.

One day while at work, a co-worker started talking

about her relationship with an ex-boyfriend. He had cheated on her several times and had had unprotected sex with other women, then come home and had sex with her. She began to cry and told me she had gone for an HIV test and was now terrified to hear the results. She was young; she had her whole life ahead of her. What if she had HIV? I listened and I hugged her; there was nothing else I could do for her but show her my support. A few days later she came to work happy and excited; her tests results were back, and they were negative. She didn't have HIV.

I was so happy for her that tears rolled down my face. I questioned her about HIV and heard all the reasons it was important to get tested. And as I listened, and thought about my own history, I realized that I, too, needed to get tested.

I was scared and ashamed, but I went to a local clinic and got tested. They asked me a lot of hard questions, and I answered every one of them. Sweat was pouring down my face and back, and I was so extremely nervous. What if I were positive? What would I say to my family? All kinds of thoughts ran though my head that as the days passed waiting for the results I began to get depressed. I was counting down the days until the nurse would call with my results.

Weeks went by and still no phone call from the nurse. I became more and more frightened and depressed. How would I take care of my son? I was so scared. Why hadn't they called? It must be bad, and they didn't want to tell me. My thoughts weren't necessarily rational, but then, fear is never rational.

I isolated myself from my family as I started making plans for the worst. I became more and more depressed. I didn't care if I took care of myself or my son. I didn't care about life, because I knew something was wrong and they were afraid to tell me.

Never Settle for Less

One morning I got off work early and headed to my grandfather's house to get my son ready for daycare. I was overwhelmed by life, tired and heartbroken. As I dressed my boy he looked up at me and said, "Mommy, don't you worry, okay?"

I smiled with tears rolling down my face. I couldn't imagine my life without him, and I couldn't imagine leaving him behind, as my mother had left me, if I really were sick. My baby gave me the biggest hug and kiss, and it felt as if someone greater than him was hugging me and holding me.

I dropped off my son at school, went home, and prayed to God to help me. I was so desperate for some relief. I called the doctor's office and asked them once again for my test results. And once again I heard that they had not arrived.

The results are really back, and they just don't want to tell me they are positive. I kept hearing that thought, over and over in my head. Finally, I couldn't take it anymore. I would just kill myself and get it over with. It would be easier than explaining to my family that because of my irresponsibility I was HIV positive. My son would be well cared for by my family. I couldn't live with this disease. It would be so much better for everyone if I just ended it now.

I reached for the bottle of pills my doctor had prescribed for me for back pain and depression and began to pour them into my hands.

Mommy, please don't do it. It was as if I could hear my son right there next to me. I dropped the pills and screamed, "God, please help me because I can't do this anymore!" I fell to the floor and asked God to forgive me for everything I had ever done wrong. "I never really meant it before," I prayed, "but I mean it now. Please forgive me." I never thought I would be in a predicament where I would want to risk it all: my life, my future, my eternity.

KESHA COX

A short time later the telephone rang. It was the doctor's office. My test results had been in the office for a week, but somehow had been misplaced. I headed right over to hear the results, praying the entire time.

When I arrived at the office I was escorted to the director of nurse's office. "Why are they sending me here?" I wondered. As I waited for the director to arrive I prayed. "Please, Lord, help me to be calm if they tell me something I don't want to hear." I was so nervous I almost passed out.

When the director finally came in, she had to call for help to calm me down so she could give me the results. "I'm so sorry for the delay," she said. "Your results are negative."

Negative!

I jumped up and down in that office and cried tears of joy. I told the director I was going to commit myself to celibacy until I was married. "That's a good choice," she replied. I knew I could do it. I promised God and myself that the next man I would give myself to would be my husband. Never again would I risk my life just because I wanted to be loved and accepted by a man. I would remember what really mattered: my life, my son, and God.

❧❦

Life was supposed to be different after the weight of my worry over HIV was lifted, but it wasn't. Weeks after receiving my results it seemed as my life was some type of Mortal Kombat game. Everything was going wrong around me. *I'm HIV negative. That's a good thing, so why do I feel so lost, so empty?* But part of me felt I was going backwards into the same old mess.

When I told a friend, she just shrugged and said, "That's part of life. Sometimes it feels that way."

It was not the answer I was looking for. I was praying and looking for answers to the war within my mind. It felt as

Never Settle for Less

if I had the devil on one shoulder telling me to enjoy life, and an angel on the other shoulder saying there was more to life that lay ahead if I would just keep pressing forward.

Family and friends thought I was losing my mind because I was asking for some type of clarity as to why I was feeling so lost. I knew God had given me another chance at life, but I was afraid of being alone. I was having nightmares about people chasing me, trying to kill me. I felt like I was hearing voices throughout the night calling my name. *What is going on is unreal. It's just your imagination playing tricks on you.* But it seemed real. My house didn't feel safe to live in. It felt haunted, filled with evil spirits.

I called my grandfather. "Daddy, can me and Kawan stay over your house for a few days because I am afraid to be home?"

"Yeah, I guess so, but remember you play by my rules," he replied sternly.

Then one evening I overheard voices downstairs, "Roscoe," the person said to my grandfather, "Kesha is losing her mind. Something needs to be done before she ends up doing something crazy."

Thoughts of suicide invaded my mind, tormenting me day and night. *Mommy, if you could hear me, please tell God to make the voices and dreams go away.*

My aunts decided to come together to do an intervention and figure out what my problems were. All I could tell them was what I was feeling inside. I was depressed, but I couldn't tell them why. My doctors were called, and immediately they wanted to run tests and place me on medication. Was I really going crazy? Was I really losing my mind? Or was I in some type of spiritual battle? I remember my grandmother saying, "When the devil wants your mind, Baby, he'll start playing tricks on you."

Kesha Cox

A few weeks later my friend invited me to a Bible study at her sister's house. Since I was able to bring my son, I agreed to go; maybe this would be an answer.

I went home from work and gave my son a bath. It was one of those evenings where everything went wrong, from the car to the furnace, to Byron calling again to argue.

I tried to call my friend and cancel, but she didn't answer her phone. I couldn't just not show up without talking to her, so finally I got into my car with my son, and I prayed. "God, please make this trip worth my while," as I headed to pick her up.

When I arrived at her house she was standing outside on her phone.

"I was trying to call you to tell you I wasn't going to make it," I told her.

"That's funny; I was on my phone the entire time and I didn't receive any missed calls."

"Oh well," I replied. "Let's go see what Bible study is all about."

When we arrived the atmosphere was so peaceful; the people were welcoming and friendly. It didn't seem real to me. It just wasn't what I was used to. Why were they so happy? Didn't they have any problems? I was amazed, but confused as well.

The minister in charge of the Bible study spoke about the love of Jesus Christ and God's forgiveness. The Word was so rich; I enjoyed every moment of it. At the end of the Bible study the minister asked if anyone wanted to give their life to Christ.

I hesitated at first; I didn't know what to except.

"The Lord says you are ready to come," he told me, and I broke down and cried. Yes, I was ready, but I was still afraid to take that next step.

He grabbed my hand and led me to Christ, right there. He read Scripture, and I cried like a baby in his arms. I felt as if the weight of life was lifted off my shoulders as the minister embraced me. There was a peaceful presence in the room that I had never felt before. "Thank you, God, for using this man to lead me to you," I prayed. I am so glad I gave my life to Christ that day, and I have been glad every day of my life since.

As I was about to leave the house, my friend's sister asked to be my prayer partner. She knew that in order for me to grow spiritually I needed the help of someone who had been in a relationship with God for a while. She became my big sister who helped me to grow in my relationship with God.

As time went on, I continued to attend Bible study and join my "big sister" in prayer each night. She gave me a study Bible and a gospel CD that I listened to every day. As I became closer to God, I still faced hardships and trials, but I was able to handle things better and differently. I ended my contacts with many old friends, including my son's father, and sold my house and moved back in with my grandfather. Trying to stay focused, and care for my son was my biggest concern. I wanted what was best for him, and if I got lonely I remembered that HIV test.

I would pray and ask God to give me the strength I needed to stay celibate and strong to care for my son, and he did just that. He gave me the strength I needed to stay focused and the resources to care for my son. That, alone, was a wonderful blessing to me.

As I continued on my spiritual journey, it seemed as if friends and family both began to turn their backs on me. I already knew certain people in my family disagreed with me, but the ones I trusted and depended on the most turned their backs as well. I was so hurt, but with time the Lord helped me to understand that some people would not understand my new walk and that I should not hold it against them.

It was hard. I loved my family, but I remembered what my grandmother said: There are some things people just won't understand, so it's best to let them be. I trusted God that he would bring us back together as a family someday.

Friends I depended on for support began to turn their backs on me because they thought I was acting strangely. But, as they were leaving, God was adding new friends to my life who would help me grow spiritually and hold me accountable for my actions. Every night before going to bed my prayer to God would be simple: "Please keep me and show me the way so that I will not fall away from You." Psalms 23 and 51 became my favorite scriptures to mediate on because I knew if I was going to change for the better it was going to take God to do the changing.

Psalm 51:10: Create in me a clean heart, O God. Renew a right spirit within me.

25. Call me David

Is what I'm feeling true, or just a fairy tale?

One night my friend invited me to a gospel concert at a church in the South Trenton Ward. I agreed; it was a Friday night, my son was two years old at the time, and I had never been to a gospel concert before. As we took our seats I was handed a flyer about a revival that was being held in Trenton the next month; the two ministers who were hosting the revival came up on stage to talk about it.

"I know him. I went to school with him," I whispered, surprised, to my friend. I didn't remember his name, but I did remember his face; on stage they called him "Minister Cox." I was shocked. He had just been a regular guy in high school. As the concert progressed, my friend introduced me to several new people. I was happy to meet them, but my son was tired and sleepy, and I knew it was time to go home.

As I was leaving, Minster Cox stopped me.

"Did you get a flyer for the revival?" he asked.

"Yes," I said, a little sheepishly, "but my son ripped it up."

He just laughed and handed me another one. "Maybe we

can stay in contact with each other if that's okay?" he said, and asked for my phone number.

Again, I was shocked. He didn't even know me. *"He can't be a real minister,"* I thought. *"Real ministers don't ask for girls' numbers. Maybe I should give him a fake one."*

But I didn't want to hurt his feelings, particularly when he first gave me his phone number.

I told him I was not looking for a relationship. All I wanted was to take care of my son. He understood. He, too, had a son of his own. I was surprised. How could a minister have a son and not be married? *Ministers,* I thought, *weren't allowed to have sex before marriage.* But I quickly learned that no one is perfect. We all fall short in some areas of our lives.

Shortly after meeting Minister Cox, he invited me for fellowship and to meet some of his friends. It was a Young Ministers for Christ revival held at the Samaritan Baptist Church in Trenton. At first I didn't plan to attend, because I didn't know what a revival was, and I was ashamed to ask him about it, but after debating with myself for several days, I finally decided to go.

There were so many people there, and everyone was having such a wonderful time singing, praising, and worshipping God. Minister Cox gave an astounding speech about a particular individual who had caught his eye and attention while he was going through certain situations in his life.

"This person must be really special to him if he is talking about her like this," I said to myself. The man went on and on about this woman—and finally I realized he was talking about me!

He even asked me to stand up in front of everyone at this revival. What had I done for this man that he would

Never Settle for Less

speak so kindly, and so highly, of me? I asked him later.

"Just being who you are and allowing me to be who I am, without judging me," he replied. "You are a listening ear and a shoulder to lean on if ever I need one."

I saw Minister Cox, who had asked me to call him David, as one of my best friends; someone who helped me and encouraged me in my walk with God. He helped me to see things from a different perspective than that of the people I had been around for many years. He challenged me to do greater things in life and apply myself so that I could become a better person and mother to my son.

The more we talked and spent time together, the more I knew that, as a woman, I didn't have to settle for less in life. I deserved better, and I was going to get better because I was determined to make a change. There were still struggles that I would have to face, and still face to this day, but I thank God for my struggles because through them I've learned valuable lessons about myself. I became stronger and wiser and a living testimony for someone else.

When I was younger, I didn't understand that if you are in a relationship with someone, that person should add to the relationship, not take from it; both should help each other become better as they strive to build their lives together.

☙❧

I remember this day so clearly; a day I would never forget. All day long I had butterflies in my stomach. David and Pastor Vaughan were attending a meeting at a church where Pastor Vaughan once worked. There had been some misunderstanding of some kind, but David never gave any details. Throughout the day I prayed for the best outcome for everyone. Finally, David called to tell me that everything was settled and the best decision was made for both Pastor Vaughan and the church congregation.

David and Pastor Vaughan were determined to make something good come out of the day; we went to dinner with Pastor Vaughan and his wife, Lady Vaughan, then headed back to their home to watch a movie. They were both such an inspiration in our lives. David and I called them our spiritual parents. My time spent with Lady Vaughan was like spending quality time with my grandmother. She was filled with much wisdom and clothed with love.

Suddenly, as we sat watching the movie, David walked toward me with a small black box in his hand and a huge smile on his face.

"Will you marry me?" he asked. I was shocked, but still managed to quickly say yes.

As he gave me the biggest hug, we all had tears in our eyes. I was so happy, I called all my friends and family that night to tell them.

Nothing could steal my happiness, and I knew that the best was yet to come. Never before had a man fully committed himself to me. Never before had a man wanted to marry me and be with me for the rest of my life. But what would my family say? I cared about their opinions, loved them, and wanted to be close to them.

The next morning I shared the good news with my grandfather. "Daddy," I said excitedly, "David proposed to me last night. He asked me to marry him."

"No one is getting married until I talk to David first," he said sternly. "Are you sure this is the right thing to do? Marriage is a big step, Kesha, you can't just pack up and leave when you get ready."

Daddy was right; I had seen how he and Mommy made it work for all those years.

There were a lot of questions and little support from my family and friends. Some felt David wasn't my type. Some felt we were rushing into marriage. Some felt I still had feelings for Byron. Everyone had an opinion. They all wanted to talk to me about it.

And I thought I'd go out of my mind.

As the questions flew, the doubts surfaced. Was marrying David something I really wanted, or was I just tired of being alone? I had to take the time to answer the questions without anyone else around. I knew that David loved me, but did I really love him?

As I prepared myself mentally throughout the engagement, I felt as if my heart had failed. I was so fearful and afraid. If I got married, that was it. I'd made my decision for life. No chance to be with anyone else. Was I ready to take on the role of stepmother? To love and accept his son? What about my son? How would the marriage affect him? Was I ready to be a family? I asked these questions and many others, but the truth was, I was gaining so much. My whole life was about to change for the better.

Philippians 4:6-7: Don't worry about anything; instead, pray about everything. Tell God what you need, and thank him for all he has done. If you do this, you will experience God's peace, which is far more wonderful than the human mind can understand.

26. Going to the Chapel of Love

*What therefore God has joined together;
let no man separate.*

The time had come for me to say, "I do." Becoming the wife of someone meant the world to me. After months of planning and consulting with my family, they were at peace with my decision to marry David. "If he makes you happy, Kesha, we are happy for you." That's all I needed to hear. Life was hard enough without having the extra tension of my aunts feeling I didn't value their opinions or concerns regarding my life.

I remember one night so clearly, when I lay in my bedroom looking up at the ceiling trying to figure out the rest of the wedding plans. Then it hit me; I would write a poem for David and my grandfather expressing my love and gratitude for them. As I grabbed a piece of paper and pen, the words began to flow from my heart till I began to cry uncontrollably.

My grandfather meant the world to me because he had

Never Settle for Less

sacrificed so much for both me and Kawan. He had loved and taken care of us; now it was time for my grandfather to rest and enjoy his life.

※

After all the planning we were anxious to walk down the aisle, but two things were still missing: a wedding date and marriage counseling. Pastor and Lady Vaughan set aside the time to have marriage counseling classes with us. I agreed with the whole process, but David was hesitant.

But Pastor Vaughan reassured him. "It's important to have and you're going to need it; trust me. After the wedding bells stop ringing, real life will hit you both hard, and if you're not ready for the challenges that will come, your marriage will end quicker than it started."

As it got closer to the date and David and I were putting the final touches together, I received a phone call from my father informing me that he was being released from prison and he would be home in time to give me away on my wedding day. My eyes lit up as if I had just seen fireworks. Everything that I dreamed of for my wedding day was finally coming together. God was releasing one tiny blessing at a time, and I was receiving each one.

※

Two days before the wedding everyone was anxious. As I was making last-minute preparations, my father called.

"Hello, my sweet sunshine, tell me what's on your pretty mind," he said, the words he had always started every phone call with. "Something has happened, and I'm not going to be able to come home until a week later."

My heart dropped. I wanted my father there, to give me away. This was the most important day of my life. He had to be there! But, I understood his circumstances and why he couldn't make it, so I assured him that I would be fine, and would be awaiting his arrival when he did get home. I had never been disappointed in my father, and I would not start now, because I knew he loved me that much.

I accepted what he had to tell me and gathered my aunts and my grandfather to tell them what had happened. My grandfather stepped right in. He would give me away, but he was worried about walking me down the aisle, because his balance was no longer good. My Aunt Kim suggested my brother walk me down the aisle in our father's place. Then, as we got closer to the front of the church, my grandfather would stand next to me and give me away. That sounded like a great idea, and my brother was more than happy to walk his big sister down the aisle. Everything was coming together.

The song *Going to the Chapel of Love* by the Dixie Cups played like a tape recorder in my head as I lay in my bed the night before my wedding, thinking about how far I'd come in life. *"No one could have kept me God, but You and I just want to say thank you,"* I prayed before sleep took me. The next thing I heard was, "Kesha it's time; it's time to get up, today is the big day, Baby." It was my grandmother's voice. I opened my eyes, and no one was in my room. "Grandma, was that you?" I smiled as I looked up to the ceiling. I felt her warm kiss touch my forehead.

"Mommy, if you can hear me I just want to thank you for being my example of what a real woman should be. I will never forget your words of love, encouragement, and wisdom. I am forever grateful for you. I love you, Mommy," I softly spoke.

"Kesha, I love you, too, and you make a beautiful bride, Baby." Again I heard these soft words within my heart.

ಖಡ

The butterflies in my stomach were flying, and my heart

was thumping. I was filled with excitement, as we drove to the church. I was going to marry a man I had met less than a year before, yet I knew he was the one. The way he made me feel was indescribable, and my heart still leaps with excitement when he looked at me and called my name.

It was a beautiful June day, the sun was shining bright, and flowers were blooming in front of the church as I stepped onto the pavement out of the white stretch limousine.

All kind of thoughts were going through my head: *What if something goes wrong?* But my bridesmaids reassured me as we gathered together into the church bookstore to pray before the ceremony. Tears of joy filled the room, even as the door opened and someone said, "Ladies, are you ready?"

Each bridesmaid and groomsman lined up to walk down the aisle to the sweet sounding voice of Lady Vaughan singing *Ribbon in the Sky* by Stevie Wonder. Then, the poem I had written for David and my grandfather began to play on the CD. I had recorded it the day before with the help of a friend.

I walked down the aisle with my brother, and there he was, waiting patiently as I walked down the aisle. I could see the tears fall from his big, brown chestnut eyes. He slowly wiped his tears away, never once turning his gaze from me.

And after twelve years of marriage I still count on those same beautiful eyes, still looking at me with love.

I am so happy I vowed to take my friend, my encourager, the one who will correct me when I'm wrong, my number one fan, David A. Cox to be my husband. On June 8, 2002, Kawan, Davon, David, and I became a family. A year later we welcomed our baby girl, Israel Katrina Cox, into the world. I am now a proud mother of three beautiful children, a wife and encouraging supporter to a loving and caring husband and pastor.

My husband and I established our first church, Calvary Fellowship Ministries, in December of 2004 in New Brunswick, New Jersey. And in September 2012, we established a second Calvary Fellowship Ministries location in Trenton, New Jersey, where I assist him in preaching and teaching the Word of God.

In November 2009 I received my associate's degree in human resources and graduated with honors, then in February 2011, I received my bachelor's degree in business administration from American InterContinental University. I am so thankful for my life, and thankful for what I had to endure and experience to be a living testimony and example for someone seeking to Never Settle for Less.

Mark 10:9: Let no one separate them, for God has joined them together.

Acknowledgements

First, I want to thank my husband, David Cox, for always being my number one fan and supporter in everything that I do. No words can describe how much I love and appreciate you for always putting the needs of our family first. You are my inspiration, and you are heaven sent. Thank you for allowing me to do what I do for others and for our family. I love you, babe.

To my loving and beautiful children, Kawan, Davon, and Israel, you are Mommy's driving force and why I pray without ceasing. You keep me on point when I'm praying for God's guidance and wisdom in your lives. Thank you for your patience in allowing me to write and complete this book. Remember: Never Settle for Less in whatever you put your hands to. You were born to win.

To my friend and my sister, Trisha King, thank you for always being a listening ear to me when I need to talk. Thank you for the support and guidance you've shown me from the beginning of this book project. You help me to see things from a different perspective, and I appreciate your honesty, patience, and your love for me.

Thank you, BJ Shores of Shooterz Photos, you are the best! To my styling team, Tiesa Johnson and Makeup by Valencia Jordan. Thank you for adding to my beauty with your creative styling techniques. Thank you, ladies.

To Kimberly Smalls, you keep me pressing beyond what I see. Thank you for keeping me on task.

To my baby sister, Myesha Price, thank you for being a

blessing to me. You did an awesome job on the book cover. I appreciate you in so many ways.

To my loving and supportive father, Derrick Hardwick, thank you, Dad, for always being there whenever I need you and most of all for your words of encouragement, wisdom, and love. I am always reminded when I hear your voice to think before I speak. You are my encourager and my hero. I love you, Dad.

Thank you, Bishop Vaughan and Lady Vaughan, for the love and support you've shown David and me throughout the years. You are such an inspiration to me, and I thank you for everything that you have given my life. You both are truly an expression of God's love.

To the one who taught me the art of storytelling, my editor and publisher Karen Hodges Miller at Open Door Publications, I knew the moment we met you were going to be the one who would help me birth *Never Settle for Less.* Thank you for your patience, expertise, and support from start to finish. You blessed my heart on this journey.

To a very special woman, Robin Dopson, who has been there since the beginning. Thank you for loving and accepting me as your own. I am forever grateful for your love, encouragement, and support.

To my beautiful aunts: Carolyn Rogers, Helen Couch (January 31, 1945 to November 20, 2014), Regina Anderson, Sheila Williams, Kimberly Stroman, and Lois James. Thank you for your love, words of encouragement, and support you've shown me throughout the years, no words can describe how much I appreciate you and value your input. You all played an awesome role in helping me with the details of this book, and I thank you and love you.

CPSIA information can be obtained
at www.ICGtesting.com
Printed in the USA
LVHW080859100122
708159LV00013B/641